THE
POPCORN
PLUS DIET

THE
POPCORN
PLUS DIET

JOEL HERSKOWITZ, M.D.

PHAROS BOOKS
A SCRIPPS HOWARD COMPANY
NEW YORK

To my parents, Reida and Irwin Herskowitz

Interior Design: Karin Batten
Cover Design: Nancy Eato

First published in 1987.

Distributed in the United States by Ballantine Books, a division of Random House, Inc., and in Canada by Random House of Canada, Ltd.

Library of Congress Catalog Card Number: 86-63177
Pharos Books ISBN: 0-88687-3029
Ballantine Books ISBN: 0-345-34400-6

Printed in the United States of America.

Pharos Books
A Scripps Howard Company
200 Park Avenue
New York, NY 10166

10   9   8   7   6   5   4   3   2   1

ACKNOWLEDGMENTS

I would like to thank the following people for their contributions to *The Popcorn*-Plus *Diet*: Ira Herskowitz, Ph.D., my twin brother, who invented the wheel (the "water wheel") and made many other helpful suggestions; Irwin H. Herskowitz, Ph.D., and Reida Postrel Herskowitz, my parents, who critically reviewed the manuscript; Debra Kaplan, R.D., M.S., my nutritional consultant, who ensured the soundness of the Popcorn-*Plus* Diet and constructed the meal plans; Raymonde Dumont Herskowitz, M.D., my wife, who shared her endocrinologic expertise and established a model for healthy family meals; Paula Gilbert, who provided support and secretarial assistance in the earliest stages of this project; Carol De Matteo, my editor at Pharos Books; and David Hendin, my longtime friend, more recently publisher of Pharos Books, who provided the structure and guidance that enabled me to turn my ideas into a book that could help others.

Joel Herskowitz, M.D.
Boston, Massachusetts
October, 1986

CONTENTS

APPENDICES

INTRODUCTION

Most people know how to lose weight. In fact, they do well for five or six days, but "blow it" the other one or two days of the week. They lose focus, lose sight of their goal, and lose control. The result is anger—at the diet that hasn't worked, and at themselves for failing (again).

The Popcorn-*Plus* Diet takes *your* knowledge and *your* experience into account. It builds upon your victories and your defeats by providing you with tools you can put to immediate use to achieve the permanent weight loss that has been so long in coming.

The Popcorn-*Plus* Diet is not a rigid prescription for weight loss, nor does it ask you to restrict your eating to popcorn or any other food. It calls upon popcorn *Plus* behavior modification, *Plus* nutritional awareness, *Plus* appropriate exercise, *Plus* specific goal setting (the key to the diet).

Rather than take a somber approach to the subject of weight loss, I have tried to present my diet in a way that is entertaining, motivating, and supportive. I trust that you will find it, as others have, effective and easy to use—loaded with principles and practices you can live with not just for the next three weeks, but for a lifetime.

1/HOW I GOT FAT AND WHAT I LEARNED FROM IT

In the spring of 1985, having experienced some winter weight creep, I set out to lose 10 pounds. Not a terribly ambitious goal, but one I felt needed to be tackled. So I gritted my teeth and began. Something unexpected happened, however. Instead of losing 10 pounds, I sailed right past my goal to lose 10 more. A total of 20 pounds in less than six weeks—effortlessly, painlessly, pleasantly.

Losing weight had never been so easy. Something special seemed to be going on here, something almost magical. I wanted to capture that and share it with others. So, as I did my daily jogging and as I drove to work, I dictated my thoughts and experiences into a portable tape recorder. I call the result the Popcorn-*Plus* Diet.

How did I arrive at this name? Clearly popcorn plays a key role. But my diet does not rely on this time-honored "fun food" in a restrictive or unhealthy way. It does indeed involve popcorn: *Plus* nutritional awareness, *Plus* behavioral measures, *Plus* exercise, *Plus*—what I consider most important of all—*specific goal setting*, the organizing force behind your weight-loss efforts.

Most of my patients and my friends would be surprised to learn that I used to be fat. In September 1968, between my first and second years of medical school, I was 5 feet 10 inches tall and weighed 195 pounds. Eighteen years later, as I write these words, I am 50 pounds lighter.

It didn't take me 18 years to lose the weight. I lost a good deal of it right away. But over the next decade or so, I suffered repeated cycles of weight loss and weight gain—and much frustration.

Through personal experience and my medical studies, I learned a lot about eating—both its nutritional and its behavioral aspects. I came to understand better how I got fat, why I continued to have a weight problem, and what to do about it.

I learned to take a step back and observe myself. I learned to laugh (or at least chuckle) at myself. And I learned to use this good-natured detachment to help me gain control over my eating behavior and weight.

Early influences undoubtedly shaped my behavior. Eating can be a form of communication between parent and child, and being a "good eater" is highly valued. So like many others, I ate to please my mother.

To make matters worse, I competed for her love and attention with an identical twin brother. That's how I learned to eat a lot of food *fast!* I barely tasted "firsts" because I was desperate for "seconds." If eating were an Olympic event, I would have been a medalist in the sprints.

I spent a chubby childhood—not "fat," mind you, but "husky." I converted the flab to height when I slimmed out as a teen. But after graduation from college I was on the road to obesity.

Unhappy with weighing nearly 200 pounds, I decided to diet. I did it the only way I knew how: distraction and modified starvation. I had nothing for breakfast, tennis for lunch, and a hamburger and salad for supper. I lost 20 pounds within several months—and my tennis improved.

My weight continued to fluctuate, however. I have never gotten anywhere near 195 pounds again. In fact, subsequent peaks have been lower and lower as I learned more about myself and about weight control.

I read widely and experimented. To paraphrase Will Rogers, I never read a diet book I didn't learn something from. Some of those I am most indebted to are listed in the Bibliography.

I learned that calories *do* count. But an arithmetical approach to weight loss is not enough. I learned that behavior is *very* important in weight control. But it's difficult to keep a food diary beyond two or three days. I learned that exercise helps. But running five miles a day will not keep all unwanted pounds away.

Most important, I learned that *I have an eating problem.* It's not bulimia or anorexia nervosa. But it's one that *has* not, and probably *will* not, go away.

I am overly sensitive to hunger. I overreact to it. Having food around stimulates me to eat. I have trouble stopping once I start. Being aware of these things has paved the way toward my gaining more comfortable and consistent control over my eating behavior and maintaining a reasonable weight.

The background, then, for the Popcorn-*Plus* Diet was recognizing and accepting the fact that I have an eating problem, which I dealt with fairly successfully through nutritional awareness and behavior modification.

The diet fell into place with the addition of two key elements—specific goal setting and popcorn. I had been aware for several years of the powerful tool of goal setting. It helped athletes set records and businessmen increase profits. It helped me immeasurably in writing a very large medical book—a four-year, 700-page project.

Like everyone else, I was aware of popcorn. I considered it okay, but I had no special fondness for it. I had a hot air popcorn maker and had done some random munching. But I hadn't yet appreciated the special value of popcorn for weight loss.

In May 1985, wishing to shed those 10 pounds, I wrote a goal statement. I put down exactly how many pounds I intended to lose by a specific date. I listed those foods I would not eat while losing weight. I read this statement aloud twice daily. This was specific goal setting.

As I put my goal statement into action, I soon discovered that having a bowl of popcorn around 9:00 P.M. kept me from "going crazy"—losing control and overeating—during supper earlier that evening.

Supper was my big meal. I tended to hold back earlier in the day, often to the point of lessened concentration, fatigue, and irritability.

Just knowing that I would have popcorn later allowed me to take smaller portions, pace myself through the meal, eat less impulsively, and permit satiety to keep abreast of my long-practiced, highly skilled hand-to-mouth coordination. I was easily able to pass up dessert and not resent my family's having it. My special treat was coming.

I also discovered a more satisfying alternative to eating apples, celery, carrots, or other low-calorie snacks during the day. Keeping a bag of freshly popped popcorn with me was an excellent way to prevent the desperate hunger that often cropped up. That made it unnecessary for me to seek food since I already had it with me. I, therefore, avoided making poor food choices. Besides, I found that the aroma released by opening up my bread bag full of popcorn generated tremendous interest and good feeling all around.

Not much magic had been associated with my previous efforts at weight loss. It tended to be hard work. But there was something special about this popcorn and goal-setting business. When a medical colleague spied a bag of popcorn poking out of my briefcase, he said, "What's that—part of a new diet?" I knew then that I wanted to tell others my story.

This book has been written to share my experiences and insights into eating, weight loss, and weight control. The Popcorn-*Plus* Diet is based upon sound and healthy principles that make it readily applicable to many people who are frustrated, overweight, and want to do something about it.

Through the use of specific goal setting combined with the thoughtful use of popcorn—a "snack food" with long-hidden nutritional value—you can now deal more effectively with the hunger that causes disorganizing and destructive desperation. It is my hope that the Popcorn-*Plus* Diet will amuse you, inspire you, and enable you to achieve success in your personal campaign against obesity.

Before getting to the particulars of my diet, let me describe some of the reasons why losing weight is important, identify some of the patterns of overeating that contribute to obesity, and introduce you to popcorn in a new light.

2/WHY LOSE WEIGHT?

The reasons to lose weight range from the far-off and intangible (increasing one's longevity) to the here and now (fitting into that suit in time for your son's wedding in two months). They also range from the physical to the psychological. In fact, the psychological suffering connected with being overweight has been called "the greatest adverse effect of obesity."[1]

Reasons for weight loss were among the issues addressed by a panel of experts convened through the National Institutes of Health in Bethesda, Maryland, February 11-13, 1985. This panel included eminent representatives from the fields of nutrition, endocrinology, internal medicine, gastroenterology, pediatrics, psychiatry, and epidemiology.

Based on this conference, the panelists developed a five-page consensus statement entitled "Health Implications of Obesity." Before looking at the conclusions and recommendations of this panel, let's consider the definition of obesity.

What is obesity? It is the state of being too fat. Fat is stored in fat cells. Obese persons have excessively large fat cells. Some also have too many fat cells. Whether this number results from early

---

[1]Wadden and Stunkard (1985). See Bibliography.

overfeeding or later overeating is not clear. The principles and methods of the Popcorn-*Plus* Diet apply in either case.

Fat provides a storehouse for excess calories. For animals whose food intake is irregular, it is particularly important, since they can never be entirely sure when their next meal will be.

Most persons in developed countries don't have that problem, however. (Parents who grew up during the Great Depression or have experienced wartime deprivation may ask, "Where are your reserves if you need them?" But this question reflects their past more than your present.)

The problem for many of us is that food is *too* readily available. We are continually being coaxed into eating. Television commercials, newspaper advertisements, and billboards bombard us with inducements to eat attractively packaged and purportedly tasty (all too often salty, sugary, nonnutritious) foods.

These assaults oblige us to eat defensively. We must become aware of our nutritional requirements, emotional makeup, and behavior. Then we can make choices based on our true needs, and not be so susceptible to media manipulation.

The difference between being *obese* and being *overweight* is not clear cut. It is generally a matter of degree. Simply stated, the obese person is fatter than one who is merely overweight.

A person who is lean, muscular, and large boned may, in fact, weigh significantly more than the so-called desirable, or ideal, weight. But such people are in the minority. (Even for the overweight person who is not "overfat," there may be significant health risks such as elevated blood pressure.)

For most of us, however, excess weight is excess fat. We're only fooling ourselves if we claim that a large frame justifies our dietary indiscretions and excess poundage.

Body fat can be measured. Specially designed water tanks are used to immerse a person for calculating the percentage of body fat. More readily available are calipers that gather a fold of skin behind the upper arm and at the waist. These values are compared to arm or waist circumference. Ratios provide a measure of fatness.

For everyday purposes, relative weight reflects relative fatness.

An estimated 34 million adult Americans, around 25 percent of persons between 20 and 75 years of age, are significantly over-weight, i.e., 20 percent or more above their desirable weight.

How do you know if you're overweight? The Metropolitan Life Insurance Company has compiled tables widely used as standards in assessing adult weight (Tables 2-1 and 2-2). These tables of "desirable" weight have been derived from data associating weight with mortality. Putting it bluntly, excess weight is linked with earlier death and lower weight with increased survival.

The data in these weight-and-height tables are not without con-troversy. The 1983 Metropolitan Life tables have been criticized because weights for men and women at the shorter end of the scale are 10 to 15 pounds greater than those on the 1959 tables.

The American Heart Association, among other organizations, has cautioned against interpreting this change as indicating that "heavier is better." The overall higher desirable weight listings

---

TABLE 2-1: Metropolitan Height and Weight Table for Women*

Height	Small Frame		Medium Frame		Large Frame	
	1959	1983	1959	1983	1959	1983
4'9"	90-97	99-108	94-106	106-118	102-118	115-128
4'10"	92-100	100-110	97-109	108-120	105-121	117-131
4'11"	95-103	101-112	100-112	110-123	108-124	119-134
5'0"	98-106	103-115	103-115	112-126	111-127	122-137
5'1"	101-109	105-118	106-118	115-129	114-130	125-140
5'2"	104-112	108-121	109-122	118-132	117-134	128-144
5'3"	107-115	111-124	112-126	121-135	121-138	131-148
5'4"	110-119	114-127	116-131	124-138	125-142	134-152
5'5"	114-123	117-130	120-135	127-141	129-146	137-156
5'6"	118-127	120-133	124-139	130-144	133-150	140-160
5'7"	122-131	123-136	128-143	133-147	137-154	143-164
5'8"	126-136	126-139	132-147	136-150	141-159	146-167
5'9"	130-140	129-142	136-151	139-153	145-164	149-170
5'10"	134-144	132-145	140-155	142-156	149-169	152-173

* Height in feet and inches, without shoes. Weight in pounds, without clothes. (Courtesy of Metropolitan Life Insurance Co.)

TABLE 2-2 Metropolitan Height and Weight Table for Men*

Height	Small Frame		Medium Frame		Large Frame	
	1959	1983	1959	1983	1959	1983
5'1"	105-113	123-129	111-122	126-136	119-134	133-145
5'2"	108-116	125-131	114-126	128-138	122-137	135-148
5'3"	111-119	127-133	117-129	130-140	125-141	137-151
5'4"	114-122	129-135	120-132	132-143	128-145	139-155
5'5"	117-126	131-137	123-136	134-146	131-149	141-159
5'6"	121-130	133-140	127-140	137-149	135-154	144-163
5'7"	125-134	135-143	131-145	140-152	140-159	147-167
5'8"	129-138	137-146	135-149	143-155	144-163	150-171
5'9"	133-143	139-149	139-153	146-158	148-167	153-175
5'10"	137-147	141-152	143-158	149-161	152-172	156-179
5'11"	141-151	144-155	147-163	152-165	157-177	159-183
6'0"	145-155	147-159	151-168	155-169	161-182	163-187
6'1"	149-160	150-163	155-173	159-173	166-187	167-192
6'2"	153-164	153-167	160-178	162-177	171-192	171-197
6'3"	157-168	157-171	165-183	166-182	175-197	176-202

* Height in feet and inches, witout shoes. Weight in pounds, without clothes. (Courtesy of Metropolitan Life Insurance Co.)

may stem from the dying off of smokers, who tend to weigh less than nonsmokers.

Another way of calculating desirable, or "ideal," body weight is depicted in Table 2-3. It is based on the following formula: for women, allow 100 pounds for the first five feet in height; add 5 pounds for each additional inch. For men, 106 pounds for the first five feet; 6 pounds for each additional inch. Add or subtract 10 percent if your frame size is large or small. Most persons should consider themselves medium and use the figure as calculated.

A widely accepted (though not universally agreed upon) guideline for excessive weight is 20 percent above the desirable (Table 2-4). This figure translates into 20 to 30 pounds for most men and women. Many persons who are only 10 or so pounds above their desirable weight may consider their weight excessive and wish to diet, too.

Which table should you use? I recommend the Metropolitan Life standards from 1959 (Tables 2-1 and 2-2) or Table 2-3. If

TABLE 2-3: Height and Weight Table*

Height	Women	Men
5' 0"	100	106
5'1"	105	112
5 2"	110	118
5'3"	115	124
5'4"	120	130
5'5"	125	136
5'6"	130	142
5'7"	135	148
5'8"	140	154
5'9"	145	160
5'10"	150	166
5'11"	155	172
6'0"	160	178
6'1"	165	184
6'2"	170	190
6'3"	175	196

* Height in feet and inches, without shoes. Weight in pounds, without clothes. After Aronson 1983.

you're 20 to 30 pounds above this figure (see Table 2-4), you're overweight.

For the truest picture, however, you must go beyond the tables. Look at, and feel, yourself. Apply the "pinch test" and assess the "jiggle factor." Pinch one of the "love handles" at your sides between your thumb and forefinger. If you hold more than two inches, you're too fat.

For the jiggle factor, put on a revealing bathing suit and have a friend watch you walk. If the flab at your sides jiggles more than a little, you flunk the test.

Have your friend photograph you from the front, back, and side. If you have a video camera, film yourself in action from several angles. Look at yourself from the neck down. Judge for yourself. Are you flagrantly fat, moderately obese, or just mildly over-

TABLE 2-4: Guidelines for Excessive Weight*

Height	Women	Men
5'0	120	127
5'1"	126	134
5'2"	132	142
5'3"	138	150
5'4"	144	156
5'5"	150	163
5'6"	156	170
5'7"	162	178
5'8"	168	185
5'9"	174	192
5'10"	180	199
5'11"	186	206
6'0"	192	214
6'1"	198	221
6'2"	204	228
6'3"	210	235

*Based on Table 2-3. Height in feet and inches. Weight, without shoes.

weight? These photographs and movies establish a visual milestone as you embark on your weight-loss program.

At this point, you've acknowledged your weight problem and should have a better idea of its degree. You hardly need a reminder that it's not healthy to be fat. But let's look now at what the National Institute of Health (NIH) experts singled out as major health risks of obesity. They include the following:

hypertension (high blood pressure)
diabetes mellitus
diminished cancer survival
shortened life span

Hypertension carries with it the increased risk of heart disease and stroke. Blood cholesterol, often elevated in obese persons, also increases the chance of cardiovascular disease. The chances of surviving cancer of the colon, rectum, and prostate are lessened for obese men; similarly, obese women have a poorer chance of surviving cancer of the gallbladder, biliary system, breast, uterus, and ovaries, than do women who are not overweight.

Longevity, too, appears affected by obesity. That's why insurance companies have become involved in making tables of desirable weight. Excess weight correlates with earlier death, and reduced weight with increased survival. If insurance companies are wary of excess weight, you should be, too.

Weight reduction is potentially lifesaving for extremely obese persons: those 100 pounds above their desirable weight or double their weight, whichever is less. Extreme obesity should be treated by an experienced physician, who will often work closely with a qualified nutritionist.

Even for the extremely obese, many of the principles of the Popcorn-*Plus* Diet will apply, nonetheless. But more extreme weight-loss measures, such as *very* low-calorie diets (closely monitored by capable professionals) or surgery may be required.

Weight reduction is also desirable for persons with a variety of other medical conditions:

> maturity-onset (noninsulin-dependent) diabetes
>
> gestational diabetes (or women who have had very large infants)[2]
>
> hypertension of unknown cause
>
> elevated blood levels of cholesterol or triglycerides
>
> coronary artery disease
>
> gout

Overweight persons with these medical disorders, among others, should pursue weight reduction *only* under medical supervision.

For many people, the psychological burden of being obese outweighs the physical. Fat people are generally looked down upon.

---

[2]Pregnancy is *not*, however, a time to lose weight!

They are sometimes considered lazy, weak-willed, and just plain unsightly.

Obese children are often cruelly teased by their classmates. Adolescents suffer isolation from their peers as they grow not just up but out. They have a tougher time being accepted at high-ranking colleges.[3] After graduation, their opportunities in the work force may be limited.

Losing weight, then, can also be a way to diminish pain and suffering. It can lead to a personal transformation that goes far beyond looking better, being healthier, and living longer. It can provide a person with more energy, a more positive attitude toward life, and the potential for greater achievement.

Are there persons who should *not* lose weight? *Yes*:

> those who are not overweight. (For them, losing weight might constitute anorexia nervosa.)
>
> those for whom weight loss is an overwhelming obsession, unbearably stressful for them and those around them.
>
> those for whom dieting and weight loss bring about significant depression.
>
> those who do not have medical clearance for actively participating in a weight-loss program.
>
> those who are pregnant.

A final point: for those of you with a family history of obesity, the cards are stacked against you. But you can succeed in losing weight. You cannot, however, continue to eat thoughtlessly, "flying by the seat of your pants." They'll become inexorably broader. For you, it is more necessary than ever to be aware of—and take charge of—your eating behavior and your weight.

The next chapter, on patterns of overeating, will help increase your self-awareness as you move toward achieving your goals.

---

[3]Wadden and Stunicard (1985). See Bibliography.

3/PATTERNS OF OVEREATING

Before looking at various patterns of overeating, let's consider the causes of obesity:

> Caloric: What you take in
> Metabolic: What you burn up
> Genetic: How you're programmed
> Behavioral: How you act

Any of these can tip the balance strongly toward obesity. This chapter will focus on behavioral aspects of eating, identifying patterns of overeating that may contribute to your weight problem.

Eating is a behavior. It begins with your sensing a need for food. An ache. A cramp. A hollowness in the stomach. A metallic taste in the mouth. A change in your ability to concentrate. Irritability. This is *hunger*.

Hunger leads first to food-seeking behavior—the hunt. Then to food preparation and selection of a place to eat. Next comes the actual process of eating.

It can be broken down into several parts:

> Portion size: How much do you put on your plate?
>
> Bite size: How much goes into your mouth?
>
> Speed: How fast do you eat?
>
> Chewing: Do you or don't you?
>
> Tasting: Said to be one of the pleasures of eating, is it one of yours?
>
> Social setting: What else do you do while you eat, and with whom?
>
> Conclusion: What brings your meal to an end? Is it when you're so stuffed it's difficult to breathe? When there's no more food to be had? When you're so disgusted with yourself that you feel like tipping over the table in anger?

Problems can crop up at each step. Over the years, I have identified, in myself and in others, patterns of overeating that lead to obesity—behaviors that interfere with losing weight and keeping it off.

As you read these descriptions, keep in mind the stages at which healthy eating behavior breaks down for you. Your awareness will provide avenues for gaining increased control of your eating behavior.

By recognizing such behavior patterns—for the most part, unconscious—you will become better able to (1) anticipate problems, allowing you to avoid or at least lessen them, and (2) gain a moment's detachment, giving you time to exercise more conscious control.

Although being overweight is not a laughing matter for most persons, a touch of humorous self-awareness can be a great help in dealing with the often overly serious business of eating (not to mention dieting).

PATTERNS OF OVEREATING

Here are several behavior patterns I have identified that can cause, or contribute to, obesity. Visualize the scenes I am depicting, and see how your behavior compares.

Mount Everest Approach

The Mount Everest Approach gets its name from a remark attributed to Sir Edmund Hilary. When asked why he climbed the world's highest peak, he replied, "Because it was there."

Why did you eat that last mound of mashed potatoes? "Because it was there." Why did you scoop out the last morsel of ice cream from the container? "Because it was there." Why did you devour the remaining hamburger on your daughter's plate? "Because it was there."

This kind of eating has nothing to do with hunger. It has to do with the presence of food. You can sit down with the best intentions, not even feeling particularly hungry, and have terrible difficulty bringing your meal to a close.

Search and Destroy Approach

Closely linked to the Mount Everest Approach is the Search and Destroy Approach. Food does not have to be visible; it just has to be available—somewhere. So, you open cabinets, refrigerators, and freezers. You discover leftovers even if they are wrapped in aluminum foil.

You cruise the kitchen like a food-sensing missile—seeking out and devouring food that your spouse (at your request) has hidden. You stop when nothing is left.

This approach is related to the widely practiced "See Food Diet." You eat what you see. The Search and Destroy Approach differs because of the aggressive, desperate quality to the hunt. Obviously, intelligent food choice is out of the question.

Last Supper Approach

With the Last Supper Approach, you have the panicky feeling that "This is it! There is no tomorrow." You'd better stuff yourself and satisfy your hunger once and for all. So you eat to the point of physical discomfort.

Desperation is also the key here. And once momentum is built up, it's difficult to apply the brakes: "I've had three hamburgers, two hot dogs, french fries, and onion rings. A couple of slices of apple pie won't make much difference, nor will a scoop or two of ice cream.''

Only One Meal Approach

The Only One Meal Approach involves only one meal indeed. But it's one continuous meal—an entire day of snacking and grazing.

This approach prevents overwhelming hunger from building up. In fact, it virtually eliminates hunger altogether, except for fleeting sensations that you're quick to act on. You behave as if you have "hungerphobia."

Gorilla Golfer Approach

Did you hear about the gorilla who hits every tee shot 450 yards straight down the fairway? Unfortunately, every putt is also 450 yards straight down the fairway.

When it comes to eating, each meal is a *big* one! Once again, hunger has little to do with continued eating.

Big Bang Approach

The Big Bang Approach has four phases. First is the "I'm-being-good" phase. Driven by your anger at being fat, you starve yourself through breakfast and lunch. Anger is replaced by hunger-induced irritability which you attempt to ignore.

Second is the reward phase. Suppertime is a blowout. You've held back all day. Now you're ready for an orgasm of eating. With blood diverted from your brain to your gut to digest this massive meal, you enter the third phase: dullness and sedation. Finally, you reach the fourth phase: guilt.

You realize you haven't solved your problem at all. You've only made it worse. You get more angry, and the cycle repeats itself.

Must Be Belgium Approach

The Last Meal and the Big Bang Approaches can be devastating when combined with the *Must Be Belgium Approach*. Remember the movie about a group of tourists frantically dashing from one country to another? It was called *If It's Tuesday, This Must Be Belgium*. The eating equivalent is "If it's lunchtime, I must be hungry."

Hunger here is not the prime mover. Conditioning is. When the time is right, long-entrenched patterns of overeating take over.

Grand Coulee Dam Approach

Ordinarily, you eat in a fairly restrained and thoughtful manner—like a well-constructed dam that allows a measured flow of water over its top at any given time.

Then, something happens to weaken the structure of your behavior. A meal at your mother's, a favorite dessert prepared especially for your birthday, a sumptuous buffet where you eat as you socialize.

Your restraint crumbles like a dam bursting. You eat like there's no tomorrow—in part because you realize there *is* a tomorrow. That's when you'll be back on your diet, gritting your teeth and depriving yourself once again of the pleasures of eating.

Deprivation is the key here. Many diets set up a rigid, unrealistic behavior pattern that you *cannot* and *will not* maintain. One way the Popcorn-*Plus* Diet helps you deal with this sense of deprivation is by advising you to carry popcorn with you during the day and to eat it when you're hungry.

Other Approaches

With the Valium, Recreational, and Texaco Approaches to eating, food is used to chase away feelings of anxiety, depression, loneliness, boredom, and emptiness. No matter how bad things are, you tell yourself, you still have your food to turn to.

With the Valium Approach, you use food as a drug to blunt unpleasant or intolerable feelings of sadness or anxiety. Mindless munching (the Recreational Approach) is often combined with equally mindless TV watching. "Filling up" to a state of physical discomfort (the Texaco Approach) can result when hunger signals are defective or absent.

Look at your eating behavior. Identify *your own patterns of overeating*. Give them names, and keep them in mind as you pursue your program for weight loss and maintenance.

ROOT CAUSES

What underlies these patterns? Hunger and desperation. Hunger is a normal part of life—a signal for seeking food and continuing to eat. But too often it triggers feelings of panic and desperation.

Think of the hungry infant, out-of-control, raging furiously. We've all been there. As a hungry adult, you don't scream and flail outwardly. But you may do so inwardly. And in your frantic desire to rid yourself of hunger—what feels like an unbearable emotional state—you make poor food choices. You select the wrong foods. You eat too much. Or both.

You may not be truly hungry at all. You may be mistaking physical or emotional discomfort for hunger. This reaction may stem from early eating experiences. As an infant, your need for warmth, physical contact, or sleep may have been misinterpreted as a need for food; and you were overfed.

As an adult, you try to quell hunger pangs resulting from physical or emotional discomfort by attacking the problem the way you're used to—by eating.

But eating offers only a temporary solution. And, when discomfort strikes again, you eat some more. That's how you got fat, and that's how you stay fat.

You recognize that you have a problem. You launch into a crash diet you found in a magazine or heard from a friend, and you lose 10 pounds in two weeks. But that weight is mostly water—and it returns with interest. You're heavier and more frustrated than ever.

You've learned a lot about dieting over the years, but no diet has successfully met your needs. The problem persists. You consider an ultra-low-calorie diet, drugs, acupuncture, and even surgery to wire your jaws shut or short-circuit your intestines. But you don't want to subject yourself to an unproven or risky method.

What you need is a *structure*—a framework for losing weight and for keeping it off. The Popcorn-*Plus* Diet provides that structure: specific goal setting. Chapter 6 will tell you how to construct a personal goal statement you can hang your knowledge and experience on to achieve the success that has been so long in coming.

The next chapter gives an overview of the Popcorn-*Plus* Diet. Subsequent chapters tell in greater detail how to lose weight and how to keep it at the level you desire.

4/THE POPCORN-PLUS DIET: HOW IT WORKS

The Popcorn-*Plus* Diet is a program for weight loss that consists of several parts:

> Nutritional awareness
> Behavioral measures
> Exercise
> Goal setting
> Popcorn

Nutritional awareness involves making proper food choices and applying the essential fact that 3,500 calories equal one pound of weight—loss or gain.

Behavioral measures are related to patterns of overeating to which many of us fall prey, often a consequence of an exaggerated emotional response to hunger.

Exercise is important as part of your overall commitment to well-being. It also burns up calories and increases your metabolic rate.

Goal setting is the framework for the diet, providing a means of maintaining your focus and motivation.

Popcorn is employed as a nutritious, low-calorie food used both during the day and in the evening. It acts biochemically on the brain to satisfy your hunger, thereby preventing panic and desperation and keeping you from making poor food choices.

THE DIET AND DIETING

An Overview

Being overweight is defined, according to standard weight-height tables, as being at least 20% above "ideal weight." Weight loss for those who follow the Popcorn-*Plus* Diet is targeted at 1 to 2 pounds a week. This is a moderate rate that gently eases your body into new and healthier eating patterns. This rate permits most persons to eat 1,200 to 1,500 calories daily.

Monitoring your weight and appearance with weight graphs and periodic photographs tells you how you're progressing. Reading your goal statement aloud twice daily keeps you on track. It reminds you of what you're giving up now (chocolate, ice cream, or beer, for example) for what you're getting: a slimmer, healthier you.

The weight-loss phase of the program is modified only slightly once you've achieved your weight-loss goal, so there's not a radical change as you move on to the maintenance phase.

Your Eating Behavior Problem

The Popcorn-*Plus* Diet begins with the recognition that you have a problem. Your problem is your eating behavior. Without this awareness, you won't get to first base in your weight control program.

You might say: "This is unfair. Why should I have to think about something that's supposed to be automatic?" For many people, appropriate eating behavior is automatic. For you, it is not. Your body's internal signals and controls have not been established, or, if they have, they don't work well. So you must employ external controls—goals, rules, and monitoring—to make up for this deficiency.

On the issue of fairness, people don't choose to have diabetes, either. But they must adhere to a special diet, take medication one or more times daily, and measure their blood sugar regularly. That lets them know how they're doing so they can lead as healthy and normal lives as possible.

Nor do people choose to have epilepsy. They can opt, however, to take their anticonvulsant medication regularly. They can reduce stresses that contribute to seizures. And, as with diabetics, they can have periodic blood tests to make sure their anticonvulsant medication is at an effective level.

So it is with your weight control efforts on the Popcorn-*Plus* Diet. You select your weight-loss goals. You monitor your progress. You observe and modify your behavior accordingly.

Disease Versus Disorder

Although you may not wish to call your obesity a *disease*, you may well have to acknowledge that you have a *disorder*. Everyone overeats now and then—the reasons are many and varied—but when your behavior *interferes* significantly with your physical or emotional well-being, you have crossed the line. You have an *eating disorder*. And it's just as real, serious, and (fortunately) *treatable* as a migraine, asthma, or depression.

Why are you overweight? There are many possible reasons, ranging from the genetic to the environmental to the hormonal. The bottom line, however, is *you have a problem*. It's up to you to do something about it.

You are overweight if you are 20 percent or more above your desirable weight. If this assessment applies to you, accept that fact and then you can begin to tackle the problem.

The next steps are provided by the Popcorn-*Plus* Diet. Built upon sound nutritional principles, the diet incorporates behavioral measures and a structured goal-setting framework with popcorn playing a key role that makes it workable and fun.

Nutritional Factors

Nutritional awareness—which includes some basic facts about calories—is essential, too. The fundamental, inescapable arithmetic is that 3,500 calories add up to one pound of fat.

Those people interested in losing weight often forget that calories are not bad. They're necessary and good. You need 1,200 to 2,000 calories a day (or more, depending on your height and activity level) to survive—even if you're lying on the beach soaking up rays. It's the 500 to 2,000 calories you eat above and beyond that which get you into trouble.

Behavioral and Emotional Issues

The patterns of overeating discussed in chapter 3 describe the emotional "triggers" that cause many persons to habitually overeat. The Mount Everest and Search and Destroy Approaches have much to do with food availability, little with true hunger. The Last Meal Approach stems from the desperate feeling that you must eat as much as possible because there may be no tomorrow. The Valium Approach is an attempt to deal with anxiety, depression, or boredom through the sedative, blunting effects of overeating. The Recreational Approach results from mindless spectating and semi-automatic food transport.

Hunger—or its absence—is crucial to these patterns. Becoming aware of true hunger versus something else gnawing at your insides (depression, ennui, or desperation) is a necessary step in gaining (and keeping) control of your eating behavior.

Goal Setting

Goal setting (Chapter 6) is the framework of the Popcorn-*Plus* Diet. It is the structure upon which you build in caloric awareness, behavioral measures, and the use of popcorn.

The process of goal setting involves establishing concrete, specific goals. You construct your personal goal statement using worksheets provided in the chapter. You write down your goals and read them aloud with feeling twice daily, visualizing your thinner self upon your target date.

In that way, you reinforce your weight-loss efforts, stay on track, and keep in mind what you're giving up—beer, chocolate, fruit juice, or other "problem" foods—for what you're getting: control over your eating behavior on your way to weight loss.

The Role of Popcorn

This well-known, lightly regarded snack is actually a highly nutritious food. Rich in complex carbohydrates and fiber, it's anything but a "junk food." Used in a thoughtful, structured way, it plays a pivotal role in the Popcorn-*Plus* Diet (see Chapter 5).

Carrying popcorn during the day allows you to respond promptly to hunger. Thus, your hunger does not lead to desperate, panicky feelings that undermine your weight-loss efforts.

Having popcorn readily available also prevents you from making impulsive, unwise food choices. Candy bars, ice cream cones, or other high-calorie foods may beckon to you, but they yield to the popcorn you're carrying.

These foods may not be strictly unhealthy from a nutritional standpoint. But they go down very quickly—and with them a lot of calories. They're not as likely to satisfy your chewing needs as several handfuls of popcorn, which takes relatively long to consume. Thus your hunger can become satisfied with less food volume and far fewer calories.

Popcorn can also be eaten before meals to blunt an overwhelming urge to overeat at mealtime, or you can have it as a midevening "mini-meal." You don't have to go "all out" at supper because you know you'll have your special treat later. And you won't feel left out while other family members have dessert. Yours is coming.

Why Does Popcorn Work?

Some of the reasons that popcorn works are clearly psychological:

reducing panic and desperation. There appear to be biochemical reasons as well.

Researchers at the Massachusetts Institute of Technology have studied the effects that some high-carbohydrate foods, including popcorn, exert on the brain. Such foods promote the release of insulin, which facilitates the entry of the amino acid tryptophan into the brain. This chemical is converted to serotonin, which acts upon centers in the brain that shut off hunger.

Popcorn and Calories

Popcorn made in an air popper has several advantages over that made with oil. One is speed. It takes less than five minutes with most poppers to produce a bowl of popcorn. With an air popper, you don't have to worry about burning oil. Nor do you have to worry about the extra calories that oil adds.

Depending on kernel size, popped corn contains 40 to 50 calories per cup. So a 200-calorie snack (equivalent to a candy bar or ice cream cone) would be 4 or 5 cups. A large bowl (up to 10 cups) is only 400 calories. During the weight-loss phase, a pinch of salt or a sprinkling of grated cheese is allowed—no margarine until the maintenance phase.

Losing Weight

You lose weight by putting your personal goal statement into action. The Popcorn-*Plus* Diet checklist keeps you on track *every day*, not just five days of the week.

The meals consist of 1,200 to 1,600 calories of balanced, nutritious food per day. A 21-day meal plan is provided in Appendix B. Meals are high in complex carbohydrates (starches), low in fats, and include healthy amounts of protein.

The day's eating plan includes 200 to 400 calories of popcorn, among other snacks. It is used as an ad lib munch, a scheduled snack (a before-dinner appetite controller), or a midevening mini-meal.

Your particular caloric allotment is determined through tables of desirable weight (see Chapter 2) and through easy-to-use calculations spelled out in Chapter 7.

Monitoring your weight and waist measurements weekly and plotting these values are critical. Graphs for doing this are provided in Appendix A. They let you know precisely where you stand. Photographs and videotapes, as well as your reflection in the mirror, give you visual feedback.

Weight loss is targeted for 1 to 2 pounds a week. More than this and you're likely to break down muscle tissue, not just fat. You're also more likely to gain back all the weight you've lost as soon as you enter a less restrictive maintenance phase.

You may, on the other hand, lose more than 1 or 2 pounds a week. The speed of loss is not crucial. What matters is establishing positive eating habits and making intelligent food choices while losing weight in a healthy and pleasant manner.

Keeping It Off

Maintenance (Chapter 8) is not radically different from the weight-loss phase. It builds upon the principles and practices you have learned and put into action.

More calories are allowed. Even desserts (in moderation) are permitted—on weekends and for special occasions. Healthy eating habits such as portion control, slowing down your rate of eating, and eating only when hungry are maintained. Physical exercise is also continued, burning up calories and contributing to overall well-being.

Again, monitoring your weight and waist regularly is as essential to keeping weight off as it is to losing weight. Graphs for recording these measurements are included in Appendix A. Periodic photographs, videotapes, and trimmer clothes provide further concrete proof of your progress.

A two-pound fluctuation from your desired weight is accepted as normal variation. Three pounds should prompt you to scrutinize your eating behavior and make whatever adjustments are necessary.

A five-pound gain triggers a return to the weight-loss phase. You then should rewrite your goal statement and set to work. You won't have as far to travel this time, since you're relatively near your goal.

Other Chapters

Chapter 10 is devoted to the Popcorn-*Plus* Diet and your children. It discusses the prevention of obesity in childhood and adolescence, how to treat it, and how popcorn fits in.

Chapter 11 consists of questions and answers. These include (1) What if you don't like popcorn or, for medical reasons, can't eat it? (2) What if you keep losing weight when you no longer want to? (3) What if you aren't losing weight on the diet? (4) Why do you tend to gain weight in the winter? (5) What should you do if you go off the diet?

Chapter 12 contains words to eat, and live, by: a collection of affirmative statements to define, describe, and inspire healthy eating behavior.

Appendices

In addition to providing graphs for monitoring your weight and waist measurements and a 21-day meal plan, the appendices (1) provide popcorn recipes and others recipes that don't include popcorn, (2) provide suggestions for healthy school lunches and snacks, (3) provide instructions for making a "water wheel" to keep track of your water intake, and (4) provide medical, psychiatric, scientific, and other references for documentation and additional reading.

That's an overview of the Popcorn-*Plus* Diet. In the next chapters, you will learn more about popcorn. You will learn how to make your own personal goal statement. You will learn how to put it into action to lose weight and keep it off. You will see how gaining control of your eating behavior and weight can be effective and fun.

Now that you've embarked on this journey, let me congratulate you on your motivation and your initial efforts. Your accomplishments will soon become apparent.

5/MEET POPCORN!

Popcorn has a lot going for it. It is crunchy, high in fiber, inexpensive, easy to prepare, relatively time-consuming to eat—all of which make it an ideal snack.

But you've got a problem and it's not just with your weight. You're not particularly crazy about popcorn. "Don't get me wrong," you say. "I like it, but it doesn't turn me on." Others say: "I *do* like it, but it's got to be salty and dripping with butter."

What *I* say is, "You haven't used it thoughtfully, as part of a structured approach to weight loss." What you need to do is— *Meet Popcorn*!

POPCORN—AN OVERVIEW

Popcorn History

The tombs of Incan leaders buried a thousand years ago in Peru contained popcorn along with gold and jewels. (You'll feel a similar devotion to popcorn, too, after it's helped you lose weight and stay slim.) After all these centuries, it still pops!

This probably wasn't the first popcorn eaten, however. Unpopped kernels, dating from 2,000 years ago, have been found in the Bat Cave in New Mexico. And popcorn estimated to be 7,000 years old has been found in caverns in southern Mexico.

Christopher Columbus made popcorn known to Europeans when he returned from the West Indies. Popcorn is said to have been part of the first Thanksgiving feast at Plymouth, Massachusetts. The brother of the Iroquois chief Massasoit brought a deerskin bag full of popcorn as a gift to the settlers, who later served it with sugar and cream for breakfast (still an excellent breakfast, but I'd suggest having it with raisins and low-fat milk instead).

Today, although popcorn is eaten widely throughout the world, most of it is grown in the United States. Americans consume nearly 10 billion quarts of popcorn every year—over 40 quarts per person.

It's big business—one billion dollars in retail sales annually. For the individual, however, it is remarkably inexpensive. A pound of popcorn costs as little as forty cents, less than a dime a quart. Low in price, low in calories—an excellent combination!

Nutritional Aspects

All popcorn is not equal. Depending on kernel size, one cup of popped corn can contain from 25 to 54 calories. I figure on 40 to 50 calories per cup. It is about 80 percent carbohydrate and 16 percent protein, with only a trace amount of fat and virtually no salt.

The high carbohydrate content of popcorn appears to play an important role in shutting off hunger signals. This effect has been linked to the elevation of serotonin levels in the brain; serotonin is a neurotransmitter that influences feeding centers in the brain.[4]

The caloric content of popcorn will also vary with preparation. Made with oil, it has 60 percent more calories: 80 versus 50. That's why an air popper is a key item in the Popcorn-*Plus* Diet. Cara-

---

[4]Wurtman (1983). See Bibliography.

mel-coated popcorn contains 106 calories per cup and Cracker Jack (which includes peanuts), 167.

Be sure you carefully read the labels of prepackaged, unpopped popcorn intended for campfire, oven, or microwave use. Some of them are loaded with oil, salt, and chemical additives.

Popcorn is high in fiber—around one gram per cup. For that reason, it has been cited as a food that may help prevent cancer of the gastrointestinal tract. Fiber also requires more chewing (slowing down your rate of eating) and provides added bulk, so you're more satisfied with fewer calories.

Why Does Popcorn Pop?

Each kernel of popcorn contains a very small amount of moisture. It is surrounded by a hard covering, the hull. When popcorn is heated to about 350 degrees Fahrenehit (177 degrees C.), the water within the kernel turns to steam. It expands and bursts the kernel open. The result of this explosion is a *Pop!*—and a kernel of popped corn.

Unpopped kernels are called spinsters or old maids. High-quality popcorn will generally give you 98 popped kernels for every 2 unpopped.

On the average, one cup of unpopped kernels expands into 30 to 35 cups of popcorn. Some varieties have been developed, however, with an expansion ratio of more than 40. That makes for some fluffy and fine popcorn!

The optimal moisture content of popcorn is around 15 percent. Much less than that and there's not enough water vapor to explode the kernel. Excessive moisture appears to weaken the kernel. This allows early release of pressure and ineffective expansion, hence, fewer popped kernels.

Popcorn is best stored in tightly-sealed glass jars. Keeping it refrigerated will also allow raw kernels to maintain their moisture content for longer periods. To restore the moisture of dried-out popcorn kernels, add one tablespoon of water per quart and seal tightly.

HOW TO MAKE POPCORN

The first popcorn probably popped by accident. Some kernels found their way into a fire and exploded their way out. This discovery led to less startling and more controlled cooking. Popcorn kernels were mixed with heated sand. That must have led to a decidedly gritty product. Later, covered pans were used to heat the kernels. Instead of sand, oil was used to bring the kernels to the required temperature.

When I was a child, the only way I knew to make popcorn was with oil. When I tried it this way as an adult, not being particularly handy in the kitchen, I made every conceivable mistake.

You're supposed to put oil into a pot, add one or two kernels, and wait for them to pop. Then you add half a cup or so of unpopped kernels, shake them around for a few minutes, and—voila—*popcorn*!

Unfortunately, I generally put in too little or too much oil. And it seemed to take forever for the oil to heat up. Sometimes, I forgot to put in the sentinel kernels. So, instead I got sentinel smoke and boiling oil.

When I finally got to put in the kernels and let them pop, the results were dismal. One-third were burned, one-third unpopped, and one-third soaked in oil.

By that time, I was so tired of waiting, so fatigued from jostling the cast-iron pot, so annoyed at the cleanup task ahead, and so dispirited by the prospect of sifting through the blackened mass for something edible that I never had the treat I'd so looked forward to.

The Miracle of the Air Popper

That all changed one day in 1984 when I saw an air popper on sale at a local department store. I took the plunge and bought it. It's turned out to be one of the best investments I've ever made!

Filling up the popcorn receptacle, I dumped in the kernels (surprisingly easy to forget), turned on the switch, and four minutes later—much to my delight—had an overflowing bowl of fluffy, hot, delicious popcorn!

What a revelation! At that point, I felt like putting a bumper sticker on my car that says: HAVE YOU HUGGED YOUR AIR POPPER LATELY? I still feel that way. This machine is a never-ending source of delight and satisfaction. It ranks right up there with the stopwatch-calculator-alarm-data-bank on my wrist that I can't do without.

Since that discovery, I have come to know the joys of making popcorn in a microwave oven. Others arrived at this insight long before I did. In fact, making popcorn ranks just behind boiling water and heating leftovers as the most frequent home use for the microwave. Unpopped kernels in a prepackaged bag or in a plastic, specially designed receptacle are put into the oven; 2 to 5 minutes later, your popcorn is ready.

Popcorn and Salt

Some people consider me a fanatic because I eat popcorn without salt. As a general rule, I keep added salt to an absolute minimum in my diet. I've found that when popcorn begins to strike me as tasteless, it's an indication that my hunger has been satisfied: it's then that I enter the phase of rote munching. I take that as a signal to bring my eating to a rapid halt.

Another reason to limit salt with popcorn is that it causes thirst, which can easily be mistaken for hunger. Furthermore, salt produces a craving for more popcorn, which makes it difficult to stop. Remember the potato chip commercial that challenges you to stop after just one chip? The same holds true for salty popcorn.

I see nothing wrong with adding a pinch of salt or a sprinkling of grated cheese to a bowl of popcorn. During the maintenance phase of the Popcorn-*Plus* Diet, you should feel free to add one tablespoon (⅛ of a stick) of margarine to a bowl of popcorn. It adds only 100 calories and contributes to taste and staying power. (Be careful even then about adding margarine . Those calories can add up!)

Keep in mind that if your popcorn doesn't strike you as good and tasty, you're probably not hungry. Therefore you shouldn't be eating popcorn—or anything else for that matter.

Now that you've met—or been reintroduced to—popcorn, you're ready to put it to use. The next chapters are devoted to goal setting—the framework for the Popcorn-*Plus* Diet—and the diet's weight-loss and maintenance phases. Popcorn recipes are included in Appendix D.

6/GOAL SETTING: THE FRAMEWORK

Eating popcorn is not all there is to losing weight on the Popcorn-*Plus* Diet. Without a plan to structure your eating, it's just another snack—maybe a better one than you might otherwise be munching on, but added calories nonetheless.

That plan is specific goal setting, the key to the Popcorn-*Plus* Diet. It provides the framework upon which you build your insights, derived from this book and your personal experience, into healthy nutrition and eating behavior.

Goal setting is a powerful, almost magical tool. It has been the organizing force behind successful accomplishment in a variety of endeavors: business, financial, and athletic. For you, the goal is personal—weight loss. The first step in achieving this goal is constructing a *goal statement*.

The *goal statement* involves the process of *visualization*—a technique used to improve concentration, as when a baseball player sees himself swinging the bat or a track-and-field athlete imagines putting the shot. Such visualization is not aimless fantasy. It is a way of experiencing the desired result before it happens, appreciating more fully what is involved, and learning how it feels to be successful.

This chapter takes you step by step through the process of constructing your personal goal statement. Using worksheets provided in this chapter, you will develop your own goal statement and write it down within the pages of this book so that it will be continuously available for your use. The next two chapters show you how to put your goal statement into action, first for weight loss, then for maintenance.

Specific Goals

The first step is to write down exactly *how many pounds you wish to lose.* It's not enough to say, "I'd like to lose some weight." You must pick a specific number. It might be 10 pounds, 40 pounds, or more. Write that number down. Use the worksheets in Figure 6-1.

Next, specify *how many inches of your waist you intend to lose.* Measure yourself with a nonstretchable tape around your midsection, using your belly-button as a landmark. This girth includes two major trouble areas. One is the "bay window" that precedes you wherever you go. The other, the "love handles" you're familiar with through assessing the jiggle factor. These are often the last vestiges of flab to go. Write the number of inches on your worksheet.

FIGURE 6-1: Goal-Setting Worksheets

Goal Weight And Waist (Fill in specific numbers):

_____ Number of pounds I will lose.

_____ Number of inches of waist I will lose.

Goal Date (Fill in):

Day of week _____ , Month _____ ,

Date _____ , Year _____ .

What I Will Give Up (Check what applies; add other foods):

_____ Ice Cream _____ Beer _____ Pizza

_____ Fruit juice _____ Soda (containing sugar)

_____ Dessert _____ Crackers _____ Chocolate

_____ Bread and butter _____ Potato chips _____ Nuts

Other foods _____

What I Will Do (Check your choices):

_____ I will drink at least 6 glasses of water per day.

_____ I will recognize that hunger is a normal sensation I'll experience from time to time.

_____ I will eat three light meals per day.

_____ I will carry popcorn with me during the day or make it in the evening to satisfy my hunger, prevent desperation, and keep me from overeating.

_____ I will weigh and measure myself at least once weekly, *and will plot these measurements.*

_____ I will exercise at least three times per week.

_____ I will read my goal statement out loud twice a day.

_____ I will visualize my thinner self daily.

_____ I will use my checklist to help keep me on track.

_____ I will take pride in my efforts and my accomplishments.

Additional Statements:_____

Put down the *exact date* you wish to achieve your goals. Be sure to include the *day of the week.* Use the calendars in Figure 6-2 to determine the precise day. This date is crucial. It provides a specific focus for your efforts. It sets your unconscious mind to work along with your conscious efforts toward your weight-loss goals.

Your Rate of Loss

Count on losing one to two pounds per week in determining that date. If you're starting on Thursday, January 1, 1987, and you wish to lose 40 pounds, write down Thursday, October 1, 1987. Your goal date may seem a long way off. But, after all, you didn't gain the weight overnight.

Losing the weight gradually will not "shock" your system. And you're much less likely to gain it all back as quickly as you lost it. What you *do* lose will be mostly fat, not water or precious muscle protein. In the process, you will have gained new, healthier eating habits. So, be patient.

If you're more than 40 pounds overweight, break your desired weight loss into 10 (or, at most, 20) pound segments. That will permit you to keep your goal more clearly in sight and experience major successes along the way.

What You Give Up For Now

Specify exactly *what you will give up* to achieve your goal. No alcohol. No desserts—except for fresh fruit. No fruit juice. No potato chips, crackers, chocolate, or other foods you're "addicted to" or have a special weakness for.

Hunger And Thirst

Acknowledge in your goal statement that *hunger is a normal sensation.* You will feel it from time to time. When you do, you'll know it's real—not boredom or thirst. You will also learn that it's brief and survivable.

FIGURE 6-2: Calendars For Goal Setting

1987

JANUARY

S	M	T	W	T	F	S
				1	2	3
4	5	6	7	8	9	10
11	12	13	14	15	16	17
18	19	20	21	22	23	24
25	26	27	28	29	30	31

FEBRUARY

S	M	T	W	T	F	S
1	2	3	4	5	6	7
8	9	10	11	12	13	14
15	16	17	18	19	20	21
22	23	24	25	26	27	28

MARCH

S	M	T	W	T	F	S
1	2	3	4	5	6	7
8	9	10	11	12	13	14
15	16	17	18	19	20	21
22	23	24	25	26	27	28
29	30	31				

APRIL

S	M	T	W	T	F	S
			1	2	3	4
5	6	7	8	9	10	11
12	13	14	15	16	17	18
19	20	21	22	23	24	25
26	27	28	29	30		

MAY

S	M	T	W	T	F	S
					1	2
3	4	5	6	7	8	9
10	11	12	13	14	15	16
17	18	19	20	21	22	23
24/31	25	26	27	28	29	30

JUNE

S	M	T	W	T	F	S
	1	2	3	4	5	6
7	8	9	10	11	12	13
14	15	16	17	18	19	20
21	22	23	24	25	26	27
28	29	30				

JULY

S	M	T	W	T	F	S
			1	2	3	4
5	6	7	8	9	10	11
12	13	14	15	16	17	18
19	20	21	22	23	24	25
26	27	28	29	30	31	

AUGUST

S	M	T	W	T	F	S
						1
2	3	4	5	6	7	8
9	10	11	12	13	14	15
16	17	18	19	20	21	22
23/30	24/31	25	26	27	28	29

SEPTEMBER

S	M	T	W	T	F	S
		1	2	3	4	5
6	7	8	9	10	11	12
13	14	15	16	17	18	19
20	21	22	23	24	25	26
27	28	29	30			

OCTOBER

S	M	T	W	T	F	S
				1	2	3
4	5	6	7	8	9	10
11	12	13	14	15	16	17
18	19	20	21	22	23	24
25	26	27	28	29	30	31

NOVEMBER

S	M	T	W	T	F	S
1	2	3	4	5	6	7
8	9	10	11	12	13	14
15	16	17	18	19	20	21
22	23	24	25	26	27	28
29	30					

DECEMBER

S	M	T	W	T	F	S
		1	2	3	4	5
6	7	8	9	10	11	12
13	14	15	16	17	18	19
20	21	22	23	24	25	26
27	28	29	30	31		

1988

JANUARY

S	M	T	W	T	F	S
					1	2
3	4	5	6	7	8	9
10	11	12	13	14	15	16
17	18	19	20	21	22	23
24/31	25	26	27	28	29	30

FEBRUARY

S	M	T	W	T	F	S
	1	2	3	4	5	6
7	8	9	10	11	12	13
14	15	16	17	18	19	20
21	22	23	24	25	26	27
28	29					

MARCH

S	M	T	W	T	F	S
		1	2	3	4	5
6	7	8	9	10	11	12
13	14	15	16	17	18	19
20	21	22	23	24	25	26
27	28	29	30	31		

APRIL

S	M	T	W	T	F	S
					1	2
3	4	5	6	7	8	9
10	11	12	13	14	15	16
17	18	19	20	21	22	23
24	25	26	27	28	29	30

MAY

S	M	T	W	T	F	S
1	2	3	4	5	6	7
8	9	10	11	12	13	14
15	16	17	18	19	20	21
22	23	24	25	26	27	28
29	30	31				

JUNE

S	M	T	W	T	F	S
			1	2	3	4
5	6	7	8	9	10	11
12	13	14	15	16	17	18
19	20	21	22	23	24	25
26	27	28	29	30		

JULY

S	M	T	W	T	F	S
					1	2
3	4	5	6	7	8	9
10	11	12	13	14	15	16
17	18	19	20	21	22	23
24/31	25	26	27	28	29	30

AUGUST

S	M	T	W	T	F	S
	1	2	3	4	5	6
7	8	9	10	11	12	13
14	15	16	17	18	19	20
21	22	23	24	25	26	27
28	29	30	31			

SEPTEMBER

S	M	T	W	T	F	S
				1	2	3
4	5	6	7	8	9	10
11	12	13	14	15	16	17
18	19	20	21	22	23	24
25	26	27	28	29	30	

OCTOBER

S	M	T	W	T	F	S
						1
2	3	4	5	6	7	8
9	10	11	12	13	14	15
16	17	18	19	20	21	22
23/30	24/31	25	26	27	28	29

NOVEMBER

S	M	T	W	T	F	S
		1	2	3	4	5
6	7	8	9	10	11	12
13	14	15	16	17	18	19
20	21	22	23	24	25	26
27	28	29	30			

DECEMBER

S	M	T	W	T	F	S
				1	2	3
4	5	6	7	8	9	10
11	12	13	14	15	16	17
18	19	20	21	22	23	24
25	26	27	28	29	30	31

1989

JANUARY

S	M	T	W	T	F	S
1	2	3	4	5	6	7
8	9	10	11	12	13	14
15	16	17	18	19	20	21
22	23	24	25	26	27	28
29	30	31				

FEBRUARY

S	M	T	W	T	F	S
			1	2	3	4
5	6	7	8	9	10	11
12	13	14	15	16	17	18
19	20	21	22	23	24	25
26	27	28				

MARCH

S	M	T	W	T	F	S
			1	2	3	4
5	6	7	8	9	10	11
12	13	14	15	16	17	18
19	20	21	22	23	24	25
26	27	28	29	30	31	

APRIL

S	M	T	W	T	F	S
						1
2	3	4	5	6	7	8
9	10	11	12	13	14	15
16	17	18	19	20	21	22
23/30	24	25	26	27	28	29

MAY

S	M	T	W	T	F	S
	1	2	3	4	5	6
7	8	9	10	11	12	13
14	15	16	17	18	19	20
21	22	23	24	25	26	27
28	29	30	31			

JUNE

S	M	T	W	T	F	S
				1	2	3
4	5	6	7	8	9	10
11	12	13	14	15	16	17
18	19	20	21	22	23	24
25	26	27	28	29	30	

JULY

S	M	T	W	T	F	S
						1
2	3	4	5	6	7	8
9	10	11	12	13	14	15
16	17	18	19	20	21	22
23/30	24/31	25	26	27	28	29

AUGUST

S	M	T	W	T	F	S
		1	2	3	4	5
6	7	8	9	10	11	12
13	14	15	16	17	18	19
20	21	22	23	24	25	26
27	28	29	30	31		

SEPTEMBER

S	M	T	W	T	F	S
					1	2
3	4	5	6	7	8	9
10	11	12	13	14	15	16
17	18	19	20	21	22	23
24	25	26	27	28	29	30

OCTOBER

S	M	T	W	T	F	S
1	2	3	4	5	6	7
8	9	10	11	12	13	14
15	16	17	18	19	20	21
22	23	24	25	26	27	28
29	30	31				

NOVEMBER

S	M	T	W	T	F	S
			1	2	3	4
5	6	7	8	9	10	11
12	13	14	15	16	17	18
19	20	21	22	23	24	25
26	27	28	29	30		

DECEMBER

S	M	T	W	T	F	S
					1	2
3	4	5	6	7	8	9
10	11	12	13	14	15	16
17	18	19	20	21	22	23
24/31	25	26	27	28	29	30

Drink at least six 8-ounce glasses of water every day to make sure thirst doesn't fool you into thinking you're hungry.

Popcorn's Function

This is where popcorn fits in. Make yourself 5 to 10 cups in the morning. Use an air popper or a microwave oven. Add a pinch of salt or none at all. No butter or margarine for now. Carry your popcorn with you—to work, to school, to a movie, to a sporting event. A plastic breadbag is perfect.

If you're hungry, drink a glass of water to make sure you're not merely thirsty. If you're still hungry after five minutes, have a couple of handfuls of popcorn.

You don't have to panic. Food is right there. Healthy, low-calorie, orally satisfying popcorn. You don't have to hunt for food or worry about making a poor food choice. You've thought it all out in advance. You're eating according to a plan that meets your needs—satisfying hunger, eliminating desperation, enabling you to lose weight.

When you eat supper, you don't have to go all-out. You know that popcorn kernels are ready to explode into action any time you want a midevening snack. While others are eating dessert, you needn't feel left out. Your "dessert," popcorn, is waiting for you. And the time it takes you to make it and eat it—it's impossible to eat popcorn quickly!—gives you further control over feelings of desperation and panic.

Monitoring Yourself

How will you know if the diet is working? *Weigh and measure yourself one morning each week. Plot these measurements* on the graphs provided in Appendix A. Photograph yourself at the start of your weight-loss program and every month or two. Videotape yourself if possible. Pinch your waist and sides between your thumb and forefinger. The grabbing will get more difficult.

These weekly measurements provide mini-goals—steps along

the path toward your ultimate destination. They help maintain your focus and your motivation.

Reading Your Goal Statement Aloud

Now that you've made your goal statement and written it down in Figure 6-3, what do you do with it? You can't close the book and expect things to happen—just as you can't merely eat popcorn and count on weight to melt away.

You must *read your goal statement out loud twice daily.* Say it slowly, thoughtfully, with feeling! Mornings and late afternoons (before supper) are best. Use your checklist (see chapter 7) to ensure that you perform this important step.

FIGURE 6-3: Personal Goal Statement

_____

_____

_____

_____

_____

_____

_____

_____

_____

_____

FIGURE 6-3: Personal Goal Statement (continued)

_____

_____

_____

_____

_____

_____

_____

_____

_____

_____

_____

_____

_____

_____

_____

Signature

_____

Date

As you say your goal statement, visualize the thinner self that's coming into being. Think of yourself from the front, back, and sides. Remember your photographs and create new ones in your mind with your mental camera. Pinch the fat at your sides and imagine how it will feel as you attain your goal. Think of fitting more comfortably into your clothes. Imagine breathing more easily as you sit while driving, working, or studying.

Needless to say, these are positively charged thoughts, which energize your goal statement with warmth and excitement.

Tape-record your goal statement and listen to it while driving or taking a break during the day. Tape a three-by-five index card with your goal weight and goal date to your bathroom mirror (or write it with a bar of soap) so that you can see it every day. Don't forget to read your complete goal statement aloud twice daily. This keeps you focused, keeps you on track.

Telling Others

Should you tell others about your specific goals? Don't. It shouldn't come as much of a surprise that you're (again) "on a diet." The difference this time should soon enough become apparent.

Do ask your family to help out. Keep trouble foods out of the pantry. If your daily routine takes you past tempting snack bars or difficult-to-resist bakeries, change your route.

If someone asks why you carry popcorn, tell them "It's a way I have to keep from getting desperately hungry." Chances are you'll meet with understanding, interest, and an outstretched hand.

Sample Goal Statement

A goal statement dated March 9, 1987:

> By Monday, August 24, 1987, I will have lost 25 pounds and 3 inches from my waist. I will not drink fruit juice, beer, or any other alcoholic beverage. I will not eat crackers, bread and butter, ice

cream, pastry, candy, or other desserts except for fresh fruit. I will drink at least six glasses of water a day. I will exercise regularly.

I recognize that hunger is a normal sensation I will experience from time to time and that it is not unbearable. I will carry popcorn with me during the day to satisfy my hunger and prevent desperation. I will make popcorn in the evening to keep from overeating at supper.

I will weigh and measure myself once weekly and plot these measurements. I will read my goal statement out loud twice daily. I will visualize a slimmer self, fitting more comfortably into my clothes, breathing more easily while driving or working. I will use my checklist every day to keep me on track. I will be pleasantly surprised at how easily the weight and inches come off.

After I reach my goal weight and waist size, I will maintain healthy eating habits through the principles of goal-setting, monitoring my weight regularly, and using popcorn or other suitable foods.

I will take pride not only in my accomplishments but also in my efforts.

Making It Your Own

Remember that this is *your* personal goal statement. Adapt my suggestions, but use any wording you like. You might, for example, choose legal language, making it a contract with yourself, or you might employ religious or athletic phrases. Do what best suits you.

Now that you've constructed your goal statement, the next two chapters tell you how to use it to accomplish your goals. Chapter 7 is devoted to weight loss, Chapter 8 to maintenance.

7/LOSING WEIGHT THE POPCORN-PLUS DIET WAY

Now that you recognize your patterns of overeating, have made your personal goal statement, and have gotten a sense of what popcorn can do for *you*, you're ready to put it all together and lose some weight.

A word of caution. Any person who is extremely obese—double his or her desirable weight or 100 pounds above it—should follow this diet (or any other, for that matter) only after medical evaluation and clearance. The same holds true for persons with acute or chronic medical conditions such as heart disease, emphysema, or diabetes.

In fact, if you have any question at all about your fitness for this weight-loss program, bring along a copy of the Popcorn-*Plus* Diet and discuss it with your physician. If you see a bag of popcorn sticking out of his or her briefcase, little explanation will be required. Feel free to modify the diet in a way that will make it safe and effective for you.

COUNTING CALORIES

Your Current Caloric Intake

The first thing to do is to calculate your current daily intake of calories. Base this on your present weight.

Allow 10 calories per pound just for basal requirements, i.e., the fuel needed for essential bodily functioning: to pump blood, to breathe, to digest food. If you were to lie in bed doing nothing for 24 hours, you'd still utilize 1,000 to 2,000 calories.

Your daily caloric needs will be greater than basal requirements, depending on your activity level. Add 20 percent for mild activity (walking between car and office; little or no other regular exercise), 30 percent for moderate activity (light exercise several times weekly), and 50 percent for heavy activity (vigorous exercise, such as aerobic running, cycling, swimming, or dancing nearly every day).

Calories for Weight Loss

To determine your daily caloric allotment during the weight-loss phase of the Popcorn-*Plus* Diet, follow Steps 1 through 7 below and in Figure 7-1.

1. Write down your current weight and multiply by 10.
2. Add 20 percent, 30 percent, or 50 percent for activity level.
3. Add Step 1 and Step 2 for your current caloric level.
4. Write down how many pounds you intend to lose and multiply by 3,500 (the number of calories per pound.).
5. Divide this figure—from Step 4—by the number of weeks over which you plan to lose weight.
6. Divide this figure by 7.
7. Subtract this number—from Step 6—from your current caloric level, Step 3.

I'm sorry if all these calculations make you feel as if you're doing your income tax. A certain amount of arithmetic is inescapable. No one, however, is going to haul you into court and ask you to document how you gained those pounds. You carry all the documentation you need with you—in the form of fat.

The final number—which should lie between 1,000 and 2,000—is your *daily caloric allotment,* the number of calories that meals and snacks will provide each day you are losing weight.

FIGURE 7-1: Calculating Your Daily Caloric Allotment

1. current weight: _____ lb x 10 = _____ cal
2. _____ cal x 20%   30%   50% = _____ cal
3. current caloric level: Step 1 + Step 2 = _____ cal
4. pounds to lose _____ x 3,500 = _____ cal
5. _____ cal from (4) divided by _____ weeks =
   _____ cal/week
6. _____ cal/week divided by 7 = _____ cal/day
7. daily caloric allotment: Step 3 _____ minus
   Step 6 _____ = _____ cal

Daily Eating Plans

Before you go any further, make sure you get an air popper (or a microwave oven), if you don't already have one. With rebates readily available, an air popper is unlikely to cost you much more than fifteen dollars. Make the investment. It'll be more than worth it. Having a popper in your possession will be concrete evidence of your seriousness. So, get one!

Three fundamental eating plans are summarized in Figure 7-2. Twenty-one days of healthy meals for weight loss to "plug in" to these eating plans are provided in Appendix B. Feel free to substitute meals that have worked for you in the past, so long as they fit your caloric guidelines.

FIGURE 7-2: Daily Eating Plans

	Breakfast	Morning Snack	Lunch	Midday Snack	Supper	Evening Snack
Time:	(6-8)	(9-10)	(11-1)	(2-3)	(5-7)	(9-10)
Plan 1	light	see text*	light	**popcorn**	light	**popcorn**
Plan 2	light	**popcorn**	light	**popcorn**	light	see text*
Plan 3	light	see text*	light	see text*	light	**popcorn**

*Pages 57 and 58

Light Meals

What do I mean by "light"? For *breakfast*, a 200- to 300-calorie meal. For example, a bowl of dry or cooked cereal with half a cup of skim milk and an orange. (*Not* a glass of orange juice. It goes down too quickly.) Be careful about granola cereals. They may have few additives, but some granolas are packed with calories—containing nearly *four times as many calories* per cup as corn flakes (see Appendix F: *Cereals*).

Or you can have two pieces of whole wheat toast (chewier than soft bread) with margarine or jam plus an apple. Cut into sections; it lasts longer. Add coffee, tea, or a grain beverage as you wish.

A light *lunch* totals 300 to 400 calories. For example, a salad of lettuce, carrots, green peppers, and cucumber with a vinegar, or lemon and spice, dressing—no mayonnaise or oil. Mix in half a can of tuna fish (3 oz) packed in water. Alternative protein sources would be 1½ ounces of American or Swiss cheese, 1 ounce (¼ cup) of uncreamed cottage cheese, or 2 ounces of chicken without skin.

Supper is a 400- to 500-calorie meal. It's equivalent to lunch with the addition of a fresh vegetable such as broccoli or green beans plus a piece of bread or small baked potato (without butter, margarine, or sour cream).

Try to have supper around 6 P.M. If you eat much later than that (more than three hours after your afternoon snack), you could be setting yourself up for a dissatisfying meal—one that leaves you hungry.

Popcorn and Other Snacks

Include 200 to 400 calories of popcorn in your diet every day. That'll be five to ten cups, which you can eat as indicated in Figure 7-1 and described more fully later in this chapter: as scheduled morning and afternoon "coffee breaks," as a carry-it-with-you nibble during the day, as a predinner appetite controller, as a mid-evening mini-meal.

For your other snacks, use cut-up fresh vegetables, such as carrots, celery, green beans, cauliflower, and peas (in the pod if possible—it'll slow down your rate of eating).

Remember that popcorn and other snacks are not "add-ons." They are an essential part of the Popcorn-*Plus* Diet, satisfying your hunger and preventing panicky, impulsive eating.

Eating Your Popcorn

The daily minimum of 200 calories of popcorn (four to five cups) will require about 2 ounces of unpopped kernels. Get acquainted with your popper and experiment with different brands of popcorn to know how much you'll need for a 200-calorie versus a 400-calorie snack.

You can eat your popcorn in any of several ways (Figure 7-2). The following plans are based on 400 calories of popcorn per day.

Plan 1. You have 200 calories of popcorn (4-5 cups) as a late-afternoon snack—a pre-dinner appetite suppressant. This leaves an additional 200 calories for a mid-evening snack.

Plan 2. You eat popcorn (200 calories per serving) as mid-morning and mid-afternoon ("coffee-break") snacks. Putting each portion into a separate bag will help you resist the temptation to power through your entire day's allotment all at once—like the Gorilla Golfer.

If having two bags around is still irresistible, leave one bag of popcorn in your car and have it on the way home.

Some people may prefer to carry a big bag of popcorn around with them to nibble as their hunger dictates during the day. Try not to eat immediately when you're hungry, though. Wait five minutes. Drink a glass of water. Chew a piece of sugarless gum. Then, if you're still hungry, eat some popcorn.

Plan 3. As an alternative, you save your popcorn until after supper. In fact, don't even make it until mid-evening—two or three hours after the meal.

Since I don't get particularly hungry during the day when I'm busy taking care of patients, I've found this last approach works especially well for me. I use other plans as well, depending on my work schedule or for the sake of variety—to maintain my enthusiasm for popcorn.

A Word of Caution

Remember that adults, too, not just children, can readily choke on half-chewed popcorn. So, slow down. Look at what you're eating. Just like snowflakes, no two kernels of popped corn are identical. Savor its aroma. Chew it thoroughly. Taking your time will allow you to appreciate its taste more fully. And your hunger will be better satisfied.

Add a pinch of salt to your popcorn if you wish, or a sprinkling of grated cheese. No margarine for now. Drink a glass or two of water with your popcorn. Ice cold seltzer or club soda adds a special touch. Enjoy it!

Other Snacks

You may be able to eat 200 or more calories per day depending on your daily caloric allotment. Have more popcorn, or choose a good-sized apple or pear. Cut it into sections and eat it piece by piece. Suck the juice out of it so it lasts longer and you taste it fully.

Keep a supply of carrot and celery sticks in a glass of water in your refrigerator. They'll be ready to greet you when you open the door. Carry some of them with you for nibbling during the day.

The frozen fruit and juice bars that have hit the market recently are terrific snacks. They're so cold that they'll keep you entertained for quite a while. And many contain only 40 calories or less. Particularly for ice cream addicts, a frozen banana (peeled and wrapped in aluminum foil) is a cool and creamy delight.

Using The Meal Plan

Once you've determined your daily caloric allotment, refer to the menus in Appendix B. Three meal plans are provided: for 1,000, 1,200, and 1,400 calories per day. These figures do *not* include popcorn (or other snacks), so you need to add 200 to 400 calories to the meal plan of your choice.

Use these meal plans as benchmarks for *your* diet. Add or subtract from the 1,000-, 1,200-, or 1,400-calorie meal plans depending on your caloric allotment for weight loss. Refer to Appendix F for caloric content of foods you'd like to include or exclude. To ensure nutritional balance, do *not* go below 1,000 calories per day.

For example, those whose daily caloric allotment is around 1,200, can use the 1,000-calorie meal plan and add 200 calories of popcorn per day. Those with a higher daily allotment of calories can have 400, or even 600, calories of popcorn daily. Choose the meal plan that best matches your caloric target.

Many people, myself included, find strict calorie-counting oppressive. The numbers here are intended to be working guidelines, not rigid rules. I suggest that you apply the *principles* of the Popcorn-*Plus* Diet (nutritional awareness, behavioral measures, regular exercise, specific goal setting, and the thoughtful use of popcorn) combined with your own experience and insights. If you're not headed in the right direction, that is, losing weight, *then* look more closely at the numbers: your daily caloric allotment, your meals, popcorn and other snacks. Make whatever adjustments are necessary.

Coffee, Tea, and Soft Drinks

Be careful with coffee, tea, and soda. Unless otherwise specified, they contain caffeine, a stimulant that can make you jittery and irritable—followed by a period of physical letdown or mental depression.

Caffeine is also a diuretic. It promotes urine flow. So you must be careful to keep up your fluid intake—at least six glasses of *water* a day. It can be tough to drink this much water if you're not used to it. Most of us aren't. So, to help you remember and to keep track of how many glasses you've had, carry a "water wheel" with you. Appendix G shows you how to make one.

Water Loss

You may be understandably pleased and excited to see that you've lost up to five pounds in just the first week. It couldn't be dehydration, you say, since you're drinking so much water—and burning up calories just running to the bathroom to void. In fact, a good deal of what you are losing *is* water.

The reason is that you are using up considerable amounts of glycogen, a bodily store of carbohydrates. With every ounce of glycogen utilized, one to two ounces of water held in your tissues are liberated. This fact probably underlies the initially rapid weight-loss many diets exploit.

The Popcorn-*Plus* Diet, does not, however, rely on water loss for its effects. It relies on your consistent application of healthy principles and practices that result in the gradual loss of *fat* through changes in your eating behavior.

Some of that initial weight loss can also be attributed to your pursuing a low-salt diet, and to clearing out your gastrointestinal tract through healthy, regular bowel movements facilitated by your drinking plenty of water and eating fiber-rich popcorn.

Don't expect to maintain the same rate of weight loss, though. Be satisfied with one to two pounds per week—a healthy amount, not too abrupt, that you've incorporated in your goal statement.

Still Hungry?

What do you do if you're still hungry? Make sure you're drinking enough water. Try eight glasses a day instead of six. Change the times of your meals and snacks. Eat your supper half an hour earlier. Make your evening popcorn as close as possible to the time you go to bed.

Be sure you're not misreading fatigue or boredom for hunger. Play the piano, listen to music, pursue another hobby, speak with your spouse, read to your children, or otherwise divert yourself to ensure that your hunger is real.

Then if you're *still* hungry, make yourself some more popcorn (4-5 cups). If this doesn't work, eat *slowly* as small an amount of chicken, tuna fish, or cheese—100 to 200 calories—as will satisfy your hunger.

Vitamins

What about vitamins? Though the Popcorn-*Plus* Diet is well balanced and not unreasonably restrictive, I recommend a daily multivitamin tablet with iron during the weight-loss phase. This provides you with a kind of "nutritional insurance."

Be careful about so-called high-potency vitamins. Don't take (without medical supervision) any that contain more than 100 percent of the recommended dietary allowance (RDA) for fat-soluble vitamins: A, D, E, and K. In contrast to water-soluble vitamins (C and the B group), they are stored by your body and can reach *highly toxic* levels.

Calcium

Most adults in this country receive less than half the recommended daily allowance of calcium. For that reason, the Popcorn-*Plus* Diet includes one or two servings daily of dairy products such as skim milk, yogurt, ricotta, or cottage cheese.

Children have special calcium needs because of their developing teeth and bones. They should have *three* servings of dairy products a day (see Chapter 10).

To guard against osteoporosis, postmenopausal women should eat at least two dairy servings daily. If milk and its products must be avoided, or if calcium supplementation is required, check with your physician. Keep in mind that calcium excess can be unhealthy, in fact, outright dangerous.

YOUR GOAL STATEMENT

The importance of making a goal statement and reading it aloud twice daily cannot be overemphasized. It keeps you on track. It reminds you what you're giving up for what you're getting. It rewards you for your efforts in gaining control of your eating behavior and your weight.

Just as important is to weigh and measure yourself weekly and record these figures on the graphs provided in Appendix A. There's nothing wrong with weighing yourself every day out of curiosity. Just don't let your spirits go on a roller-coaster ride as your weight undergoes normal fluctuations, up to two pounds in either direction. Keep in mind also that by exercising regularly you will be replacing fat with muscle. So, your waist measurement may drop even though your weight has not. Your persistence will win out. Stick to the plan.

THE CHECKLIST

To make sure that you're doing what it takes to lose weight, use the Popcorn-*Plus* Diet checklist (figure 7-3). Space is provided for you to add items of importance to you. For example, "I did not have ice cream" or "I did not drink beer." Use a yellow marker to highlight the item you are concentrating on each week.

Before you fill it in, make several photocopies so that they'll be available in future weeks. Or design your own. Then, use it!

FIGURE 7-3: The Popcorn-*Plus* Diet Checklist

Week of Monday ————————— **through Sunday** —————————

	Mon.	Tues.	Wed.	Thurs.	Fri.	Sat.	Sun.
I read my goal statement twice aloud.							
I visualized my thinner self.							
I drank ____ glasses of water. (fill in)							
I ate popcorn to prevent panicky eating and poor food choices.							
I ate light meals.							
I exercised for 20 minutes or longer.							
I avoided problem foods.							
I weighed myself and plotted the measurement.							

Week's starting weight ———— lbs. Week's ending weight ———— lbs.

EXERCISE

What about exercise? Exercise allows for greater loss of fat than muscle when dieting. It also burns up calories that contribute to excess weight.

Perhaps most importantly, exercise appears to increase your metabolic rate even when you're not exercising. That helps you counteract your body's tendency to *lower* its metabolic rate—burn food more slowly—during periods of weight loss. That's why caloric deprivation without regular exercise tends to produce agonizingly slow weight loss (if it's successful at all).

For these reasons, exercise is an essential part of the Popcorn-*Plus* Diet. Running, walking, swimming, and cycling at a gentle pace are fine. The role of exercise is discussed in greater detail in chapter 8.

NOT WORKING?

What should you do if the diet is not working? Reread this chapter and the preceding one on goal setting. Make sure that you are reading your goal statement aloud twice daily (*with feeling*) and using the checklist. Even if you are not yet losing weight, at the very least you are building healthier eating habits. And this behavior is bound to pay off in time.

Consider cutting your daily caloric intake down by 200 to 300 calories. Women shouldn't go below 1,000 calories per day, men 1,200. If over two or three weeks you're still not losing weight, consult with your physician. You might have an underactive thyroid. You might be depressed. You might be pregnant. Get yourself checked!

There's a good chance that you'll achieve your goal weight and waist measurements well before your goal date. Congratulations! You can celebrate now—and again when you arrive at that date.

In the meantime, don't let your commitment slacken. Gently liberalize your diet along the lines set forth in the next chapter. And keep reading your goal statement aloud twice daily.

8/KEEPING IT OFF:
YOUR NEW GOAL

Now that you've lost the weight, what next? Record your new look by taking some pictures. Get out of your roomy clothes and buy some that fit. Congratulate yourself. You're ready for the maintenance phase.

This is where many diets break down—the transition from weight-loss to keeping-it-off phases. With the Popcorn-*Plus* Diet, however, the move is not abrupt. You're already eating three healthy meals a day. You have a better sense of what foods and patterns of eating behavior get you into trouble. You're eating popcorn in a planned, thoughtful manner—warding off desperate hunger and avoiding unwise food choices.

Since you no longer need to lose weight, you can add 200 to 300 calories (perhaps even more) to your diet. Have an occasional beer or glass of wine. Don't be misled by ''lite'' beer commercials. You may save 50 calories per glass, but 12 ounces still contains around 100 calories.

Go ahead and have that piece of chocolate cake if you wish. But restrict desserts—a single portion only—to weekends or special occasions.

This chapter tells you how to figure your caloric maintenance, discusses the role of exercise, and, of course, describes how popcorn fits in.

Eat: You're Entitled

Being fat has many negatives attached to it in our society. It is only natural, therefore, that what got us fat—eating and food—should take on some of these negative associations. The most extreme consequence of such negative feeling is anorexia nervosa, an intense fear of fatness.

But food and calories are *not* bad. They're necessary and good—at least as good as you make them. The same holds true for eating. You're entitled to eat. In fact, it's a biologic necessity.

Calculating Your Caloric Maintenance

Remember that if you were to lie in bed doing nothing for 24 hours, your body would still require 1,200 to 1,500 calories for basic, life-sustaining activities. That's your basal level of calories. But it's not these calories that get people into trouble. It's the calories they pile on top that get them fat and keep them fat.

Keep these guidelines in mind:

Your first 1,200-1,500 calories.......Go ahead......... (green light)
Your next 300-600 calories............Be careful .... (yellow light)
Beyond that....................................Stop! ....(red light)

Identify your own comfort, caution, and no-go zones. As discussed in Chapter 7, calculate your basal caloric level by multiplying your desirable weight (the goal weight you've achieved) in pounds by 10. For a 120-pound woman that would be 1,200 calories, for a 160-pound man 1,600.

As before, your daily caloric allotment for maintenance will depend on your activity level (see Figure 8-1). So add 20 percent for mild activity, 30 percent for moderate activity, and 50 percent (or more) for heavy activity. Since you're now at your goal weight, you no longer have to adjust your daily caloric intake downward.

FIGURE 8-1: Daily Caloric Allowance

Activity Level	Basal Calories	Additional Calories	Total Calories
For 120-pound Woman:			
Mild	1,200	240	1,440
Moderate	1,200	360	1,560
Heavy	1,200	600	1,800
For 160-pound Man:			
Mild	1,600	320	1,920
Moderate	1,600	480	2,080
Heavy	1,600	800	2,400

Fifteen hundred calories, then, is a reasonable starting point for lighter persons, 2,000 calories for those who are heavier. You can continue to use the meal plans in Appendix B for healthy, well-balanced meals for maintenance, not just for weight loss.

Differences in Metabolic Rate

I repeat: *These figures are just guidelines.* You may find you can handle more calories without gaining weight. Or you may use the lower target level, keep an accurate calorie count, and *still* add pounds.

I've experienced this personally and could swear I had an underactive thyroid. In fact, I arranged for blood tests to check my thyroid function. Alas, it was normal. The harsh reality is that my maintenance level of calories is no more than 2,000 calories, despite running several miles daily. So I must continue to watch my food intake carefully.

The difference appears to lie in one's metabolic rate as well as one's activity level. Some people simply burn off calories more easily than others.

We all know persons who seem able to eat anything and everything without gaining a pound. Others like you and I merely have to breathe deeply near a bakery to put on weight. So you may

have to subtract 200 or more calories from your calculated daily
maintenance to determine your true caloric maintenance level.

Importance of Monitoring

Continuing to monitor your weight and waist is *critical* for maintaining your weight loss. It's the most objective form of "feedback" you have to let you know where you stand. But it's not
enough to make these measurements, nor is it sufficient to write
them down somewhere.

You must plot these values. Use the graphs in Appendix A, or
make your own. Then open your eyes so you can see and accept
what the numbers are telling you.

How often should you weigh yourself? Once a week for purposes of plotting. But you should feel free to do it more often to
maintain a high level of awareness and prevent sneaky increases
in weight.

Gaining Weight

A two-pound fluctuation from your goal weight is acceptable as
normal variation—particularly in women who retain fluid during
some phases of their menstrual cycle. Some pizza here, some Chinese food there and your weight increases. You'll unload the salt
and accompanying water within a day or two, though. So don't
get upset.

A three-pound gain should cause you to stop and ask yourself
some questions. "What's going on here?" "Am I holding back during the day and pigging out at supper?" "Am I drinking enough
water?" "Am I really hungry when I eat?"

Make sure you're drinking six to eight glasses of water a day.
Observe your eating behavior and food choices more carefully.
Keep a food diary for two or three days, writing down everything
you eat.

Sometimes, just increasing your level of awareness in this
way will allow for rapid self-correction. Make whatever adjustments you need to. At this stage, they are likely to be relatively
minor.

A five-pound weight gain should press you into immediate action. Return to the weight-loss phase. Use the goal-setting worksheets in Chapter 6 to write a new goal statement. Use the checklist. Chances are that you're a lot closer to your goal than when you started out. Go for it!

Popcorn and Maintenance

What about popcorn while you're maintaining your weight? You can continue eating popcorn as discussed in Chapter 7: nibbling at various times during the day, scheduling morning and afternoon snacks, or having a midevening mini-meal.

You can also experiment. Have popcorn for breakfast with your usual cereal or by itself, combined with milk and fresh fruit. It's different and delicious! Try some of the popcorn recipes in Appendix D.

Feel free to add a bit of margarine to your popcorn. One table-spoon per 200-calorie portion is fine. But keep in mind that two such servings a day add 200 calories. That amounts to 1 to 1½ pounds a month, or around 20 pounds for the year—just due to "a bit of margarine" alone. So, be careful!

Keep your popcorn maker out on the counter, ready for action. It will facilitate your popcorn making and, at least psychological-ly, block your path to the refrigerator, where foods less appropri-ate than popcorn may be lurking.

BENEFITS OF EXERCISE

There are many reasons to exercise. It reduces stress and makes you feel good. It allows you to replace sagging fat with lean, con-toured muscle. It reduces your risk of heart attack. It increases your metabolic rate so your caloric allowance for maintenance may actually rise. It uses up calories that otherwise would "join the family" as fat.

Exercise also helps to structure your eating behavior. It's best not to eat for an hour or two before exercising. You certainly won't want to eat while you exercise unless you're running an ultramarathon, nor for an hour or so afterward.

Kinds of Exercise

What kind of exercise is best? That's a matter of individual preference. It also depends on your physical condition.

If you are not currently exercising regularly (three or more times per week) and vigorously (fast walking, jogging, or swimming, for example), ask your physician to review your exercise program and provide you with medical clearance—especially if you are over 35 years of age.

As suggested by Dr. Kenneth Cooper, the founder of the aerobics "movement," select an activity that appeals to you enough to want to do it for years, if not a lifetime, i.e., swimming, cycling, cross-country skiing, walking, jogging, or running. Running is defined as anything faster than a nine-minute-per-mile pace. You should exercise three to five times per week, 20 to 30 minutes at a time.

Exercise should leave you, at most, feeling mildly, *pleasantly* fatigued. If it leaves you exhausted, cut back on the intensity or the duration of the exercise, not the number of sessions a week. Be sure to keep up your fluid intake. Particularly on hot days, you may need to drink 8 to 10 glasses of water.

Burning Up Calories

It's not just vigorous exercise that burns up calories. Walking slowly (at 2 mph) burns up 3 calories per minute. Walking more briskly (4 mph) utilizes 5 calories per minute. These figures compare with around 10 calories per minute for running or swimming.

Keep in mind that exercising regularly and vigorously will not in itself prevent you from gaining weight. I learned this firsthand when my weight crept up despite running three to six miles a day.

It's taking in too many calories—*eating*—that puts on the pounds. As you pursue your exercise program, remember, too, that a single can of beer or a candy bar adds as many calories as running a mile or two burns off (see Appendix F: Caloric Content of Everyday Foods).

There's still more you can do to consolidate your gains—or, should I say, your losses. The next chapter presents further behavioral tools for weight control, additional tips for everyday eating.

9/BEHAVIORAL TOOLS FOR MAINTENANCE

Now that your weight is where you want it to be, take a step back. Look at what you've done to bring about the change. Consider what you can do to make your achievement long-lasting.

Adding to the principles and practices set forth in Chapter 8, this chapter gives you further tools that you can use to keep your weight at the desired level.

Portion Control. Get a sense of what is a reasonable amount of food to put on your plate. Develop a feel for what constitutes a 200- to 300-calorie portion. Three or four ounces per meal of meat, fish, or other high-protein food are as much as is needed for healthy nutrition.

You don't need to buy a scale. Cut a pound of uncooked hamburger meat or steak into four equal pieces. Keep one for yourself and freeze the other three immediately, unless, of course, you're preparing food for others, too. Remember that less meat means less fat—and fewer calories.

Slowing Down. Eating more slowly allows chemical signals to reach your brain to let you know your hunger is being satisfied. Chew your food well, but don't get hung up counting the number of times you chew. Try to be aware of the taste and texture of what you're eating.

Put your fork down between bites. At the very least, don't "load up" again until you've swallowed what's in your mouth.

Use your hands and mouth for something other than eating. Wipe your face with a napkin. Sip some water. Get out of your seat and help serve. Clear the table. (Make sure others are done first.) Speak to others at the table. Look at them—and away from your plate—when you do.

Reading an engrossing book can also slow you down. Be careful, though. It might get you into mindless eating—the Recreational Approach with a book instead of a TV.

What's Left? When you're faced with a small amount of food left on your plate after your hunger has been satisfied, **stop!** Consider your options.

You can have it later as a midevening snack. You can include it in your salad for lunch tomorrow. You can put it in your compost pile. You can give it to your dog. Or you can eat it.

Don't.

Social Eating. Beware of stand-up eating: cocktail parties, picnics, and buffets. One nibble per conversation may seem fine. But multiply this by 10 or 15 and you've consumed a lot of food without even noticing it. And dinner may be yet to come!

Instead, pick out a few of the fat-drenched, calorie-laden "appetizers" that appeal to you most and eat them without guilt. Have 400 or 500 calories' worth. Let *that* be your meal.

Remember that appetizers tend to be salty and make you want to eat more. Drink water instead. Hover around the crunchy salad items—cauliflower, carrots, peppers, and the like—and go easy on the high-calorie dips.

Alcohol. Be very careful about alcohol. A single beer, six ounces of wine, or a two-ounce cocktail contains 100 to 150 calories. Limit yourself to one drink. Then hit the seltzer or sugar-free soda.

Salad Bars. I love 'em. But you've got to resist the economic and gastronomic temptations to stuff yourself. Limit yourself to two platefuls. Avoid creamy, sugary, caloric dressings in favor of oil-and-vinegar or yogurt-based dressings.

Instead of a "bottomless salad bowl," choose a "side salad."

Traveling. Eating away from home can disturb anyone's routine. Until modern technology develops a collapsible popcorn maker, it'll be difficult to pack one in your suitcase.

You can, however, fill a couple of bread bags with popcorn and take them with you. Day-old popcorn doesn't get soggy. In fact, it has a delicious, "aged" flavor all its own.

Diet Composition. What should your diet consist of? It is becoming clear that a diet relatively high in complex carbohydrates (starches) and low in fats is healthiest—less likely to promote heart disease among other problems. Sixty to 70 percent starches and 25 percent fats are reasonable proportions to aim for. The meals that make up the 21-day meal plan (Appendix B) are built along these lines.

Try to include fish in your diet once or twice weekly. Bake it or broil it. Frying may double or triple the caloric content. Fish is a good source of protein with very little fat. It also appears to contribute to prevention of cardiovascular disease because of special oils it contains.

Remember Pavlov. Pavlov observed that food presented to an experimental animal will make it salivate in readiness for eating. If a bell is rung *as* food is presented (or *just before*) over several trials, salivation can be elicited subsequently by ringing of the bell alone. Such conditioning can play a powerful role in many aspects of *our* eating behavior as well.

Our environment holds many triggers (like the bell) that can get us to salivate and think that we're hungry. In fact, they can induce *real* hunger pangs. Driving by the "golden arches" of McDonald's or passing by a bakery can trigger reflexes that prepare us for eating. That makes putting our money down, consuming the product, and gaining weight all the easier.

So remember: like it or not, there's a lot of that salivating dog in each of us.

Food Rewards. Do not, in general, reward yourself with food. But don't be so uptight that you can't enjoy a special treat now and then.

Stay In Control. If you're at an ice cream parlor and can't resist—there may be no particular reason why you should, especially if it's a weekend day—go for the small or medium cone rather than the hot fudge sundae or large cone.

Don't act impulsively. Think for a moment before selecting an apple versus a piece of cake, popcorn versus a hunk of cheese.

Staying in control doesn't mean depriving yourself. It *does* mean—*MAKING CHOICES.*

Be aware of *why* you are eating:

> *hunger:* a necessity
> *pleasure:* all right to a degree
> *emotional distress*: not a successful nor long-term solution, and one which is likely to make you fat permanently

Hunger and Waiting. If you're hungry during the day, try not to eat popcorn, or anything else, immediately. Drink a cup of coffee or a glass of water. Chew a piece of sugar-free gum. Get involved in an activity. Wait 5 or 10 minutes. If you're still hungry, *then* eat something.

This pause helps to remind you what real hunger is, and it gives you time to make a thoughtful food choice.

Hobby or Job. If afternoons or evenings are unstructured times that lead you to mindless eating, take up a hobby. Or seek a part-time job that gets you out of the house. Aerobic exercise, particularly in a group setting, is a terrific pastime. It's time structuring, calorie expending, and health enhancing.

Too Thin, They Say. You will undoubtedly hear from friends and family members that you've lost too much weight. You are a far better judge of this, however, as you stand naked in front of a full-length mirror. You may not wish to invite your critics in with you for a viewing; but come bathing-suit time, you can rest your case.

You will come to appreciate what a remarkable job clothes manufacturers do in making people look thin—often a lot thinner than they actually are!

A Reminder. Now that you're in new clothes that fit you comfortably and well, you may still feel a bit of tightness around your waist—especially when sitting.

Don't take this as a signal that you're still fat. Let it remind you, though, that continued vigilance is necessary.

Heavy Load. Every now and then, take a winter jacket and fill the pockets with stones that total the weight you've lost. Or, select a pile of your heaviest books; make them equal the weight you've lost, and carry them up a flight of stairs that you climb regularly.

You'll be amazed, truly staggered, at how much extra baggage you used to carry around. You won't want to gain it back after this little demonstration.

Lapses. Accept the fact that you'll occasionally fall back into old patterns of overeating. Don't get too angry at yourself. Mount Everest doesn't go away. It's always there. But so, too, is your commitment to healthy eating behavior and your overall health.

Continue to weigh and measure yourself regularly. Plot the values on your graph. Don't blink away any upward trends.

Short-Term Goals. Set monthly or seasonal weight goals. Write down your desired weight and the target date on a three-by-five index card. Place it on your bathroom mirror or the sun visor of your car so you can see it every day. Change the location of this message from time to time so you continue to notice it.

Attention Ex-Smokers. I'm sure that some of you reading this book are former smokers. You have successfully shed your cigarette addiction but find that you're gaining a couple of pounds or more per year (or per month). And you're unhappy about it.

First of all, congratulations on quitting. You have profoundly improved your health by shaking an insidious and dangerous habit. The Popcorn-*Plus* Diet will help you to gain, or to regain, control over your eating habits. Anyone who has conquered the "evil weed" can do it!

With these additional tools for maintenance, you're better equipped to carry your weight control program successfully into the future. In the next chapter, you will learn how you can—and why you should—influence the nutritional future of your children as well.

10/THE POPCORN-PLUS DIET AND YOUR CHILDREN

Is there anything wrong with being fat as a child? Yes, plenty—unless you enjoy being called "Fatso," "Tub-a-Lard," "Mr. Big," or any of the other less-than-endearing names children so readily use on one another.

Being fat sets a child apart. It keeps him or her out of the mainstream. And its damaging emotional effects may carry over into adulthood.

Does obesity in childhood promote fatness in later life? Apparently so. Forty percent of obese children and 70 percent of obese adolescents grow up to become obese adults.

The reasons are not clear. Genetic factors appear to play a major role. Early overfeeding may also. Fat cells stimulated to multiply early in life persist into adult years. They may demand to be filled. But not only fat cells are laid down in childhood. *Habits* are, too—behavior patterns that can be crucial in determining later obesity.

It's not just calories that are of concern in a child's diet. Sweets can destroy teeth. And fat-laden foods rich in cholesterol may pave the way for later heart disease.

In summary, there appears to be quite a lot wrong with being fat as a child.

PREVENTION

What can you do about the problem of obesity and your children? The first step is prevention. You can't start developing healthy eating habits too early.

If your infant is crying, don't assume he or she is hungry. Learn the difference between the needs for warmth, cuddling, and food. In doing so, you'll avoid conditioning your child to interpret all physical and emotional discomfort as hunger. You may well prevent later patterns of overeating, such as the Valium and Texaco Approaches (see Chapter 3).

When you children are older, continue to foster healthy eating habits. Don't make them clean their plates. Let *them* learn when their hunger is satisfied. Instill in them an awareness of *hunger* versus *appetite*. Appetite is more of a "head" response to the environment—often a result of conditioning or advertising—than a "gut" feeling that stems from true nutritional needs.

Encourage your children to eat a variety of foods. Have them taste unfamiliar vegetables or fruits. Don't bribe them with money or dessert. Don't overdo fruit juice. Most contain over 100 calories per eight-ounce glass.

Children should drink three glasses of milk or the equivalent per day. This provides calcium needed for growing bones and teeth. Don't allow them to guzzle milk to slake their thirst, though. Too many calories! Let them discover how satisfying a glass of cold water can be.

Sugar

Be especially careful about breakfast cereals. Read the labels. Sugar is the first or second most abundant ingredient in many cold cereals. (Salt is usually high on the list as well, with coloring agents not far behind.)

Such cereals can be cloyingly sweet, loaded with sugar that causes a craving—divorced from hunger—for more food. So read the labels carefully. Don't let artificial colors, cartoons, contests, or other come-ons seduce your child (or you) into choosing an unhealthy product.

Cooked cereals, which usually contain less sugar (and salt) than cold cereals, are easy and quick to prepare. They're particularly good for cold mornings and for a change of pace.

Cutting down on sugar may improve your child's behavior. Although not scientifically proven, parents often report that reducing sugar in the diet diminishes irritability and leads to fewer temper tantrums. The exaggerated ups and downs of their child's behavior are smoothed out.

Education

Teach your children about the basic food groups: carbohydrates, proteins, and fats. If *you* don't know, consult a nutritionist, or go to the library and look up some of the references listed in the Bibliography for this chapter.

Explain to them the difference between complex carbohydrates (starches), like those contained in pasta and whole grain breads, and simple carbohydrates (sugars), like those in cookies and other sweets. Teach them about calories—why they're necessary (as fuel) and how they can make you fat.

Point out that low-volume, high-calorie snacks, such as candy bars or potato chips, often contribute to obesity in childhood and adolescence. Contrast these with high-volume, low-calorie snacks such as popcorn or carrots, that are better for the teeth as well as the waistline. A list of recommended snacks is included in Appendix C.

Teach them to be tolerant and understanding of persons who might have a weight problem. (See the book by DeClements in the Bibliography.)

Adolescence

Chubbiness in early adolescence can be normal. That flab around the middle may well disappear as the growth spurt proceeds. Don't assume that your son or daughter will grow out of it, however. Discuss with them eating habits that contribute to obesity. Rather than losing weight, it may be more appropriate for your child to maintain his or her weight for six months to a year. Discuss this option with your pediatrician.

During the teen years, "junk food" often reigns supreme. Encourage your children to try to make intelligent choices—not to pick foods impulsively, based on availability alone or what's "in."

Exercise and Television

Get your children into the habit of regular exercise. Team sports such as football or basketball can be a great thrill, but "carry-over" sports—those that can be pursued actively at any age (swimming, running, walking, cycling, and tennis)—should be encouraged.

Limit television watching. Scientific evidence suggests that TV watching is a major contributor to the increased incidence of childhood obesity in this country. Not only is this a time of relative inactivity, but many children "snack out" while watching TV. Furthermore, they come under the influence of advertising for candy bars and excessively sweetened, chemical-laden breakfast cereals.

Setting An Example

Nine out of 10 obese children have obese parents—their role models. Develop positive eating habits in your children by demonstrating them yourself and expressing them in action day in and day out. By following the Popcorn-*Plus* Diet, you're setting a healthy example for them to follow.

Helping your children develop good eating habits does not mean making them neurotic about getting cancer because they "garbaged out" at a birthday party. It does mean, however, showing them the importance of making healthy choices. Letting them know that what goes into their mouths enters their bodies and minds, influencing their mood, thought, and behavior.

Husky, Overweight, or Obese?

Is your child overweight? You may be able to tell by referring to standard growth charts (Figures 10-1 through 10-4*) or simply by looking.

Use these tables to determine your child's height and weight percentiles. If they match—say, both at the 25th or both at the 75th percentile—that's fine. But if the weight is one or two percentile curves greater than the height—at the 90th for weight versus the 50th for height, for example—he or she is significantly overweight.

For children who are well into adolescence (girls 15-16 years, boys 17-18), use the height and weight tables in Chapter 2. Weighing 20 percent or more above the desirable weight indicates a significant problem (see Figure 2-4).

If you find these tables confusing, if your child falls into a "gray" area, or if you have any question whatsoever, share your concerns with your pediatrician.

Using the Popcorn-Plus Diet

If you think your child has (or might have) a weight problem, bring along a copy of the Popcorn-*Plus* Diet and discuss it with your pediatrician. He or she may organize a weight-loss program right there, or may refer you to a nutritionist experienced in working with children.

Adapt the principles and methods of this book to suit your child's needs. Pick out realistic goals and meals. (See Appendix C

---

*From the Department of Health and Human Services, Public Health Service, National Center for Health Statistics, Division of Health Examination Statistics, Hyattsville, Maryland.

FIGURE 10-1: Height for Age (Girls: 2-18 Years)

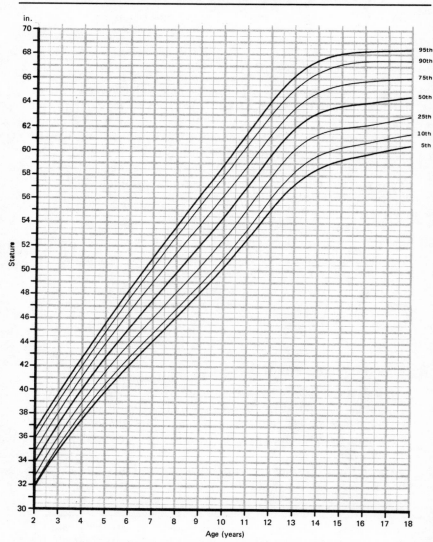

Figure 10-1: At the 50th percentile, half the 10-year-old girls are taller than 54 inches; half are shorter.

FIGURE 10-2: Weight for Age (Girls: 2-18 Years)

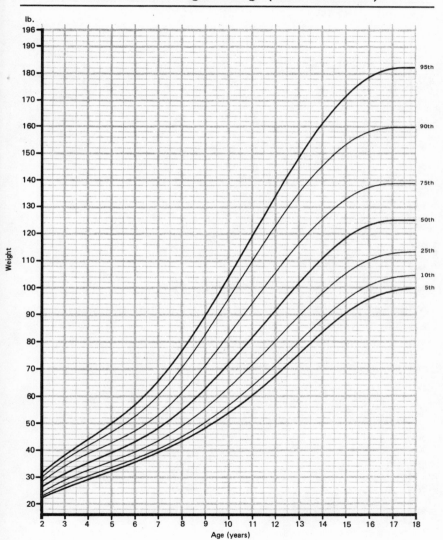

Figure 10-2: At the 50th percentile, half the 10-year-old girls weigh more than 72 lbs.; half weigh less.

FIGURE 10-3: Height for Age (Boys 2-18 Years)

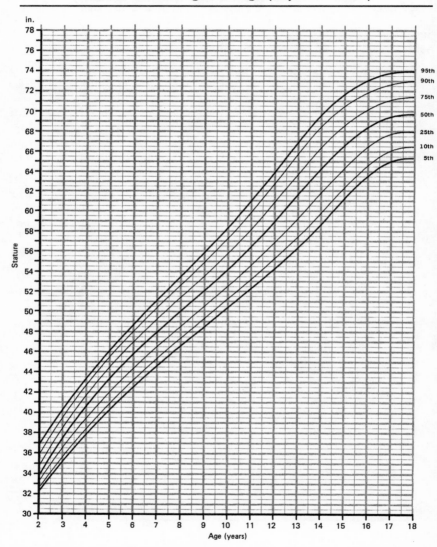

Figure 10-3: At the 75th percentile, one quarter of 11-year-old boys are taller than 58 inches; three quarters are shorter.

Figure 10-4: Weight For Age (Boys 2-18 Years)

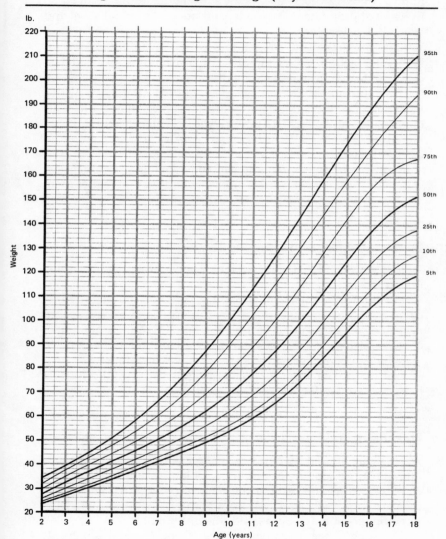

Figure 10-4: At the 75th percentile, one quarter of 11-year-old boys weigh more than 89 lbs.; three quarters weigh less.

for school lunches and snacks.) It can be quite difficult to determine a child's caloric needs. There's no simple formula. An effective and appropriate diet will depend upon your child's age and stage of development.

Take care that losing weight does not become a focal point for family interaction. Such a tug-of-war (particularly with an adolescent) can lead to a *serious* eating disturbance.

The Popcorn-*Plus* Diet can help avoid such destructive tussles by enabling your child to achieve greater control of his or her eating behavior and weight. (At the very least, you can help by keeping "trouble foods" such as ice cream, cookies, and corn chips out of your home.)

Involve your son or daughter in constructing a personal goal statement. Make weekly measurements and plot them. Let them see and feel what's being accomplished.

Popcorn For Everyday Use

Even if your child is not overweight, popcorn can still play a role in daily life.

It is an ideal after-school snack. Let your son or daughter discover that large amounts of salt are not needed to make popcorn tasty and satisfying, nor is butter necessary. Use a small amount of cholesterol-free, low-salt margarine (regular or diet), if you wish.

Include popcorn instead of sweets in the school lunch bag for a special treat.(Watch out for snacks disguised as healthy granola bars.) See Appendix C for other snack ideas.

Preventing Problems

When your children eat popcorn, make sure they don't stuff handfuls into their mouths at one time. This can lead to dangerous choking and aspiration into the trachea (windpipe). Picking up popcorn with one hand only (not both), or with no more than three fingers at a time, is a good rule of thumb.

If your child *does* choke on a piece of popcorn and coughs, *do not pound him or her on the back.* Don't reach into the mouth to remove the food. This can move an object from the throat into the trachea. Or it can cause a partially blocked windpipe to become more fully obstructed.

Coughing itself is highly effective in reopening a blocked airway. If, however, your choking child (1) is not coughing, (2) cannot speak, (3) shows increasing respiratory distress, or (4) is not moving air at all, administer four back blows between the shoulder blades. This can be followed by the Heimlich maneuver or chest thrusts, if necessary.

If these efforts reopen the airway (and lead to coughing or normal speaking), stop, take a step back, and observe. If they do not work the first time, repeat two or three times. If they still don't work, call for help.

I suggest that children younger than four years of age not be allowed to eat popcorn.

Talking, laughing, or running while eating popcorn (or any other food) is dangerous. Make sure your children don't do it.

Also, they should eat only kernels that are fully popped. Otherwise, they could damage their teeth. (The old wives' tale about unpopped kernels winding up in the appendix, blocking it, and causing appendicitis appears to be just that—an old wives' tale.)

Keeping these safety measures in mind, your children—like you—can enjoy the many pleasures and health benefits of popcorn.

Laying the groundwork by fostering healthy eating habits in your children, you can derive satisfaction from establishing patterns of eating that can last a lifetime. And you can feel glad that you'll be sparing them many of the miseries you've experienced yourself.

11/ANSWERS TO DIETERS' QUESTIONS

Is exercise really necessary?

For weight loss: No. For maintenance: No. For optimal health and well-being: Yes.

Even with chronic disabling conditions, it should be possible, with your physician's help (plus that of a physical therapist in many instances), to construct an exercise program that meets your needs.

For cardiac patients, a walking program may be suitable. For those who suffer from arthritis, a swimming program. There are potentially tremendous benefits to be gained through regular exercise. So try it!

I've tried popcorn, and I really don't like it. Is there something I can use instead?

If popcorn is not for you, or you have a medical condition, such as an irritable colon, that prevents you from eating it, substitute an appropriate high-carbohydrate, low-salt snack. Rice cakes are ideal. They contain only 30 to 40 calories apiece. So you can eat five or six of them instead of four to five cups of popcorn for your 200-calorie snack.

Puffed-wheat and puffed-rice cereals are other excellent alternatives. Like popcorn, they are nutritious and consume time while you consume them.

Don't forget about raw vegetables (such as celery, carrots, radishes, and cauliflower) and fresh fruit (apples, pears, and watermelon). They're crunchy, refreshing, and filling.

The key is not popcorn so much as it is the structure of the Popcorn-*Plus* Diet—goal setting and the thoughtful use of appropriate snacks—combined with your commitment.

Can the Popcorn-*Plus* Diet be used in a group setting?

Yes, with great effectiveness. Although it has been designed for the individual dieter on his or her own, the Popcorn-*Plus* Diet works well in a supportive group setting.

Group approaches such as Weight Watchers and Diet Workshop are of proven benefit. But not everyone has the time, money, or babysitting facilities to pursue weight control in this manner. Many people have successfully lost weight on their own. The Popcorn-*Plus* Diet provides the tools for many more to do the same.

Group sessions can be a tremendously positive part of your weight-loss program. Weekly meetings provide an opportunity for mutual inspiration, motivation, and support. They are also helpful for identifying problems you might be overlooking or underemphasizing.

When should I start?

Start anytime. Now, for example. If you're under a lot of stress and don't think this is a good time, however, hold off—but lay the groundwork. Get yourself an air popper. Buy some popcorn. Construct a goal statement, but don't put it into action yet.

If the Christmas and New Years holidays are coming and you

know this will be a tough time for you, start eating the Popcorn-*Plus* Diet way. Eat a little less dessert than usual—no seconds, for sure. Keep your alcohol intake down. Emphasize crunchy, low-calorie snacks (such as popcorn) and appetizers—not calorie-packed, fat-drenched nibbles.

Make choices. You'll be getting in the groove. And when you're ready, you'll *really* be ready.

What if I keep losing weight and I don't really want to?

The first thing I would say is, maybe you *do* really want to. After struggling for so many years and finally discovering something that works, you're naturally inclined to keep on doing what makes you feel good. Success is hard to turn your back on.

But *don't* keep on going. It can only make you ill. Use the sense of control you have developed, and switch over into the maintenance phase. It should not be a difficult transition.

Add a few hundred calories. Eat some dessert. Add a little margarine to your popcorn. Make a goal statement that's specifically tailored for maintenance, and put it to use.

Many medical and psychiatric conditions are associated with weight loss. They include diabetes, hyperthyroidism, cancer, colitis, brain tumor, anorexia nervosa, depression, anxiety, and AIDS.

Don't self-diagnose. If you continue to lose weight two or three weeks beyond achieving your goal and entering the maintenance phase, go to your physician for a checkup.

Should women and adolescent girls take iron?

In general, unless you have a history of iron deficiency anemia, it's probably not necessary. I do, nonetheless, suggest that you take a multivitamin with iron during the weight-loss phase as a kind of "nutritional insurance." Avoid "high-potency" preparations for the reasons give in Chapter 7.

Do include legumes, green leafy vegetables (such as spinach), liver, whole-grain and iron-enriched cereals and breads as often as possible within your diet. Iron absorption is enhanced by vita-

min C. So make sure you regularly eat citrus fruits and such vegetables as tomatoes, broccoli, and green peppers.

If your menstrual periods are too frequent, overly long, or associated with heavy flow, consult your physician. He or she may
wish to check your CBC (complete blood count) and iron level.

What if I can't lose weight?

Reread chapters 6 (on goal setting) and 7 (on losing weight). Make
sure you are drinking at least six glasses of water a day and that
exercise is part of your weight-loss program.

You may be one of those rare persons who truly *does* have a
metabolic problem, such as hypothyroidism or Cushing's disease.
It's more likely that your basal metabolic rate is relatively low,
though not abnormal. You're so efficient in using the calories you
take in that you need to lower your daily caloric allotment. Discuss these possibilities with your physician or a nutritionist.

Maybe you're pregnant. If there's any chance you might be,
have a pregnancy test. You don't want to deprive your developing
baby of essential nutrients. Plan on renewing your weight-loss efforts after pregnancy and nursing.

Maybe you're depressed or anxious. Depression can affect your
appetite and cause weight gain *or* loss. (In some instances, dieting
and weight loss themselves can cause depression.) You might be
anxious about becoming a more attractive person—thrust into sit-
uations you don't yet feel prepared to handle.

Maybe your spouse doesn't want you to change. Perhaps you're
afraid of being a smaller person—one who literally "carries less
weight." Fat does form a protective shield. It keeps people away.
Its persistence may reflect fears of intimacy and anger.

To look into these emotional factors, consult with a qualified
psychiatrist, psychologist, or social worker. For some persons,
group therapy may be particularly suitable.

What about medications?

Except for vitamins with iron taken during the weight-loss phase,
medications have no place in the Popcorn-*Plus* Diet.

Drugs such as amphetamines (including Dexedrine) or phenylpropanolamine may assist in short-term weight reduction. But weight is often regained after the pills are stopped. And they carry risks of headaches, dizziness, insomnia, high blood pressure, and addiction.

Taking diuretics (water-losing pills) makes no sense at all. Weight loss then is, truly, only water loss. Flowing out in the urine is potassium, too. So a person on diuretics may suffer from dizziness and irregular heart rhythm.

Your goal is not a "quick fix" to your problem. There is none. Your goal is to *change your behavior*—to develop and maintain healthy eating habits through your own insights and efforts so that your weight loss will be long-term.

I seem to gain weight every winter, no matter what I try. What should I do?

This appears to be a common pattern. Perhaps it has to do with your body's needing a bit of added insulation during the cold months. Or you may be experiencing a *seasonal affective disorder*. Persons with this problem tend to become depressed and to gain weight under circumstances of reduced sunlight. The physiologic basis for this pattern is yet to be fully understood. It appears to be mediated through hormones that affect the brain and influence mood and appetite.

What you can do is to dress warmly (though comfortably) indoors as well as out. Adjust your winter weight goals accordingly. You might choose, for example, to maintain your present weight through the cold months until spring.

Accept the fact that your metabolism may change depending on the season. Look forward to shedding those extra pounds during the warmer months. The therapeutic benefits of artificial light are currently under investigation. If you experience significant depression, consult a psychiatrist or other mental health professional.

What should I do if I go off the diet?

Don't get too angry at yourself. A lapse or two is not going to undo all the good things you've set in motion. Don't make your situation worse by collapsing into the Grand Coulee Dam Approach (see Chapter 3).

Try to pinpoint where things went wrong. Ask yourself, Am I putting too much food on my plate? Is my family supporting me, or are they undercutting my efforts? Am I weighing myself regularly, plotting the measurements, and truly understanding what they tell me? Am I drinking enough water?

Get back on the diet. Pick up where you left off. Make a new goal statement if you need to. Use the answers to the above questions to help you get back in control and stay on track.

12/WORDS TO EAT (AND LIVE) BY

1. I drink at least six glasses of water a day.
2. I exercise at least four times a week for 20 minutes or longer.
3. I carry popcorn with me to prevent hunger and desperation.
4. I try to eat when I'm hungry, and *only* when I'm hungry.
5. I weigh myself once a week and plot this measurement on a graph.
6. If I'm five pounds or more overweight, I write a new goal statement and put it to use immediately.
7. I don't get overly angry at myself for lapses. I simply resume healthy eating habits.
8. I do not eat to the point of feeling stuffed.
9. I eat desserts only on weekends or special occasions.
10. I eat portions of reasonable size.
11. I need 1,500 calories for maintenance and don't apologize for eating this much.
12. When I eat popcorn, I know I'm doing something good for myself.
13. I won't be more satisfied with ten chocolates than one. So I just have one, enjoy it, and spare myself the calories and the anger.
14. I try to eat slowly so that I can readily appreciate when my hunger is satisfied.

15. I eat popcorn in the late afternoon to help avoid overeating at supper.
16. I keep "trouble" foods like crackers, pretzels, and dry-roasted nuts out of the house.
17. I eat a diet high in starches and low in fats.
18. I don't go all-out at supper because I can look forward to a satisfying bowl of popcorn later in the evening.
19. I make food choices thoughtfully, not impulsively.
20. I use humor to keep from getting too serious about eating.
21. If popcorn doesn't taste good to me, I know I'm not hungry.
22. I use water, sugarless gum, patience, and food to deal with hunger.
23. I set monthly and seasonal weight goals.
24. I don't bribe my children with sweets.
25. I photograph myself periodically to gain a truer perspective of my appearance.
26. I try to sort out hunger from thirst or emotional distress.
27. I write down my goal statement and say it out loud twice a day.
28. I use my checklist to help keep me on track.
29. I try not to load my fork until I've swallowed what's in my mouth.
30. I drink alcoholic beverages in moderation, or not at all.
31. I encourage my children to participate regularly in vigorous physical exercise.
32. I carefully read the ingredients of foods that I buy my children.
33. I teach my children to satisfy their thirst with water rather than soda, fruit juice, or milk.
34. I don't assume that a crying baby is hungry.
35. I try to instill healthy eating habits in my children by setting a good example.
36. I'm losing weight because I like myself, and I will like myself even more when I reach my goal.
37. I take pride in my efforts and my accomplishments.

Add statements of your own that describe and affirm your commitment to healthy eating behavior.

APPENDIX A: Weight And Waist Graph

Current Weight Date ———

Weight

Goal Weight Date ———

Month	1	2	3
Week	4	8	13
Waist Size	—	—	—

Use this graph to track your weight and waist measurements. At the top left, mark your starting weight and the current date. Near

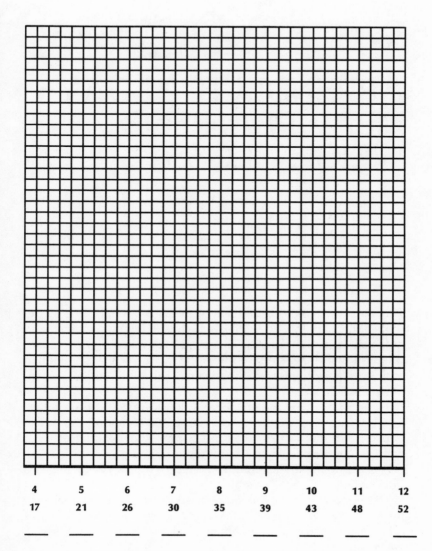

4	5	6	7	8	9	10	11	12
17	21	26	30	35	39	43	48	52

___   ___   ___   ___   ___   ___   ___   ___   ___

the bottom left, indicate your goal weight and target date. Weigh and measure yourself once weekly and *plot these measurements*.

APPENDIX B: 21-DAY MEAL PLAN FOR WEIGHT LOSS

This appendix contains 21 days of meals for weight loss as described in Chapter 7. These meals are low in fat, high in fiber, and nutritionally well balanced. This meal plan was designed in consultation with Debra N. Kaplan, M.S., a registered dietitian and staff nutritionist at the Joslin Diabetes Center, Boston, Massachusetts.

Three meal plans are included: 1,000 calories, 1,200 calories, and 1,400 calories per day. Add 200 to 400 (or more) calories of popcorn per day as described in Chapter 7, depending on your daily caloric allotment for weight loss.

Feel free to make substitutions. Refer to Appendix F to help you in choosing other food combinations.

These meals can, of course, be used during your maintenance phase as well as for weight loss. Add an appropriate number of calories to reach your maintenance caloric level. See Chapter 8 and Appendix F.

Recipes are provided in Appendix E for items marked with an asterisk.

DAY 1

1,000 Calories	*1,200 Calories*	*1,400 Calories*

Breakfast

1,000 Calories	1,200 Calories	1,400 Calories
½ grapefruit ¾ cup shredded wheat ½ cup skimmed milk	½ grapefruit ¾ cup shredded wheat ½ cup low-fat (1%) milk 1 slice toast 1 tsp margarine	same as for 1,200-cal diet
Calories: 186	303	303

Lunch

1,000 Calories	1,200 Calories	1,400 Calories
8 oz skimmed milk 2 slices whole wheat bread ½ cup Tuna-Apple Salad* 1 cup cut-up raw vegetables, zucchini, green pepper, cucumber	same as for 1,000-cal diet: substitute 8 oz low-fat (1%) milk	same as for 1,200-cal diet, but with large green salad with 2 tsp corn oil plus vinegar as desired
Calories: 348	378	478

Supper

1,000 Calories	1,200 Calories	1,400 Calories
1 serving Baked Mini-Meat Loaf* 1 cup mashed potatoes ⅔ cup broccoli 1 tsp margarine	same as for 1,000-cal diet with 2 tsp margarine	same as for 1,200-cal diet with 1 cup fruit: fresh or water-packed
Calories: 500	534	614
Total: 1,034	1,215	1,395

DAY 2

1,000 Calories	*1,200 Calories*	*1,400 Calories*

Breakfast

4 oz orange juice	4 oz orange juice	same as for 1,200-cal
½ English muffin	1 English muffin	diet
½ tbsp peanut butter	1 tbsp peanut butter	

| Calories: 172 | 290 | 290 |

Lunch

large salad: lettuce,	same as for	same as for 1,000-cal
tomatoes, onions,	1,000-cal diet	diet with 2 oz
cucumbers, green		pita pocket bread
pepper, mush-		
rooms, radishes,		
alfalfa sprouts		
with		
2 oz Swiss cheese		
1 oz turkey meat		
1 tbsp Italian dressing		

| Calories: 379 | 379 | 529 |

Supper

1 serving Beef with	same as for	same as for 1,200-cal
Chinese-Style	1,000-cal diet	diet with ¾ cup
Vegetables*	with 1 cup	applesauce,
⅔ cup cooked white	total cooked	5 Arrowroot
rice	white rice	cookies in
½ cup unsweetened		place of
applesauce		graham
2 squares graham		crackers
crackers		

| Calories: 434 | 502 | 596 |

| *Total:* 983 | *1,171* | *1,415* |

DAY 3

1,000 Calories	*1,200 Calories*	*1,400 Calories*

Breakfast

1,000 Calories	1,200 Calories	1,400 Calories
¼ cup low-fat cottage cheese 1 slice whole-wheat toast 8 oz skim milk	⅛ honeydew melon 1 egg (not fried) 1 slice whole-wheat toast 8 oz low-fat (1%) milk	same as for 1,200-cal diet
Calories: 187	316	316

Lunch

1,000 Calories	1,200 Calories	1,400 Calories
3 oz hamburger patty hamburger roll lettuce, tomato, onions 1 tbsp catsup	3 oz hamburger patty hamburger roll lettuce, tomato onions 1 tbsp catsup	same as for 1,200-cal diet with 1 cup minestrone soup
Calories: 416	416	499

Supper

1,000 Calories	1,200 Calories	1,400 Calories
3 oz broiled sword-fish 1 cup asparagus 1 small baked sweet potato 1 tsp margarine 8 oz skimmed milk	4 oz broiled sword-fish 1 cup asparagus 1 small baked sweet potato 1 tsp margarine 8 oz low-fat (1%) milk	same as for 1,200-cal diet with 1 small dinner roll and 1 tsp margarine
Calories: 418	494	613
Total: *1,021*	*1,226*	*1,428*

DAY 4

1,000 Calories	*1,200 Calories*	*1,400 Calories*

Breakfast

1 cup Yogurt Fruit Crunch* made with 1 cup Grape-Nuts, 1 cup fruit (fresh or water-packed)	1 cup Yogurt Fruit Crunch* made with 1 cup granola, 1 cup fruit 8 oz Alba sugar-free hot cocoa	same as for 1,200-cal diet
Calories: 203	306	306

Lunch

2 slices pizza 14" diameter 1 cup salad: lettuce, tomatoes, cucumbers, green pepper 1 tbsp Italian dressing	same as for 1,000-cal diet	same as for 1,000-cal diet with 1 oz grated cheese
Calories: 416	416	516

Supper

4 oz roasted chicken without skin ½ cup cooked peas ½ cup butternut squash 1 tbsp Italian dressing	same as for 1,000-cal diet with ¾ cup peas ¾ cup squash 1 tsp margarine green salad	same as for 1,200-cal diet with 1 medium apple
Calories: 423	519	600
Total: 1,042	*1,241*	*1,422*

DAY 5

1,000 Calories	*1,200 Calories*	*1,400 Calories*

Breakfast

1,000 Calories	*1,200 Calories*	*1,400 Calories*
4 oz orange juice or 1 medium orange Oatmeal Muffin*	4 oz orange juice or 1 medium orange Oatmeal Muffin* 1 tsp margarine 4 oz low-fat (1%) milk	same as for 1,200-cal diet
Calories: 200	295	295

Lunch

1,000 Calories	*1,200 Calories*	*1,400 Calories*
1 cup tomato soup 1 medium tomato stuffed with 3 oz drained canned salmon mixed with 1 tbsp diet mayonnaise and chopped onion 4 saltines	same as for 1,000-cal diet	same as for 1,000-cal diet with 2 oz whole-wheat pita pocket bread
Calories: 399	399	501

Supper

1,000 Calories	*1,200 Calories*	*1,400 Calories*
1 serving Baked Fish with Creole Sauce ⅔ cup cooked okra green salad ⅔ cup cooked rice 8 oz skimmed milk 1 tbsp Italian dressing	same as for 1,000-cal diet except with 2 servings fish	same as for 1,200-cal diet with 1 small dinner roll plus 1 tsp margarine
Calories: 417	508	627
Total: 1,016	1,202	1,423

DAY 6

1,000 Calories	*1,200 Calories*	*1,400 Calories*
	Breakfast	
2 Whole Wheat Pancakes*	½ grapefruit	same as for 1,200-cal diet
1 tbsp maple syrup	2 Whole Wheat Pancakes*	
	1 tbsp apple butter	
	1 tbsp maple syrup	
Calories: 210	283	283
	Lunch	
2 slices whole-wheat bread	same as for 1,000-cal diet: substitute	same as for 1,200-cal diet with 3 oz turkey
2 oz sliced turkey lettuce, tomatoes, onions, alfalfa sprouts	8 oz low-fat (1%) milk	1 medium apple
8 oz skimmed milk		
1 tsp mayonnaise or 2 tsp imitation mayonnaise		
Calories: 352	376	502
	Supper	
4 oz boiled lobster	same as for 1,000-cal diet with 1 dinner roll	same as for 1,000-cal diet with 1 cup New England clam chowder and 4 saltines
1 medium baked potato		
⅔ cup broccoli with 1 oz Cheddar cheese melted on top		
2 tbsp sour cream		
Calories: 433	518	644
Total: 995	*1,177*	*1,429*

DAY 7

1,000 Calories	*1,200 Calories*	*1,400 Calories*

Breakfast

½ whole-wheat bagel ½ tbsp cream cheese 8 oz skimmed milk	1 whole-wheat bagel 1 tbsp cream cheese 8 oz low-fat (1%) milk	same as for 1,200-cal diet
Calories: 187	323	323

Lunch

3 oz baked haddock ⅔ cup rice ⅔ cup cooked broccoli 1 tsp margarine 1 medium apple	same as for 1,000-cal diet	same as for 1,000-cal diet with 4 oz haddock, 2 tsp margarine
Calories: 397	397	472

Supper

1 serving Chicken Cacciatore* ½ cup spaghetti 3 tbsp Parmesan cheese ¼ cup low-salt tomato sauce ⅔ cup broccoli 1 tsp margarine	same as for 1,000-cal diet 1 cup spaghetti	same as for 1,200-cal diet with large salad plus 1 tbsp Italian dressing
Calories: 420	493	598
Total: *1,004*	*1,213*	*1,393*

DAY 8

1,000 Calories	*1,200 Calories*	*1,400 Calories*

Breakfast

1,000 Calories	1,200 Calories	1,400 Calories
½ small banana ½ cup Grape-Nuts Flakes 8 oz skimmed milk	½ small banana 1 cup Grape-Nuts Flakes 8 oz low-fat (1%) milk	same as for 1,200-cal diet
Calories: 208	290	290

Lunch

1,000 Calories	1,200 Calories	1,400 Calories
omelette prepared with 2 eggs, chopped onions, green pepper, mushrooms, 2 tbsp low-fat milk, 1 oz Cheddar cheese, 1 tsp margarine (for pan) 1 oz pita pocket bread	same as for 1,000-cal diet	same as for 1,000-cal diet with 1 English muffin plus 1 tsp margarine
Calories: 403	403	497

Supper

1,000 Calories	1,200 Calories	1,400 Calories
3 oz hamburger patty 1 tbsp catsup ½ cup corn ½ cup mashed potatoes 1 tsp margarine	same as for 1,000-cal diet 1 cup corn	same as for 1,200-cal diet with 1 oz American cheese for cheeseburger
Calories: 433	509	615
Total: *1,044*	*1,202*	*1,402*

DAY 9

1,000 Calories	1,200 Calories	1,400 Calories

Breakfast

1,000 Calories	1,200 Calories	1,400 Calories
1 English muffin with 1 oz part-skim mozzarella cheese melted under broiler	½ grapefruit 1 English muffin made with melted cheese and 1 tsp margarine	same as for 1,200-cal diet
Calories: 207	319	319

Lunch

1,000 Calories	1,200 Calories	1,400 Calories
2 tbsp peanut butter 3 triple Rye-Krisp crackers 1 cup cut-up vegetables 1 medium apple	2 tbsp peanut butter 2 slices whole-wheat bread 1 tbsp jam or jelly 1 cup cut-up vegetables	same as for 1,200- cal diet with sliced banana added to sandwich
Calories: 369	402	507

Supper

1,000 Calories	1,200 Calories	1,400 Calories
4 oz halibut broiled with 1 tsp margarine ½ cup cooked carrots ⅔ cup rice 8 oz skimmed milk	5 oz halibut broiled with 1 tsp margarine ½ cup cooked carrots ⅔ cup rice 8 oz low-fat (1%) milk green salad plus 1 tbsp Italian dressing	same as for 1,200-cal diet with 1 orange
Calories: 395	540	600
Total: 971	1,261	1,426

DAY 10

1,000 Calories	*1,200 Calories*	*1,400 Calories*

Breakfast

4 oz orange juice or 1 orange 1 egg scrambled with Pam 1 slice whole wheat toast	same as for 1,000-cal diet with 1 additional slice whole-wheat toast, 1 tbsp jelly or preserves	same as for 1,200-cal diet
Calories: 196	312	312

Lunch

2 oz pita pocket bread stuffed with ¼ cup tuna mixed with 1 tsp diet mayonnaise, 1 oz part-skim mozzarella cheese, ⅔ cup cut-up steamed broccoli 8 oz skimmed milk	same as for 1,000-cal diet with 8 oz low-fat (1%) milk	same as for 1,200-cal diet with 1 medium apple
Calories: 382	412	493

Supper

1 serving Beef, Beans, and Macaroni Chili* ½ cup cooked green peas 1 cup peaches, water-packed	same as for 1,000-cal diet with 1 small dinner roll	same as for 1,200-cal diet with 2 tsp margarine
Calories: 448	533	601
Total: 1,026	1,257	1,406

DAY 11

1,000 Calories	1,200 Calories	1,400 Calories

Breakfast

1,000 Calories	1,200 Calories	1,400 Calories
1 cup fresh fruit: melon balls, grapefruit and orange sections ½ cup low-fat (1%) cottage cheese 3 triple Rye-Krisp crackers	same as for 1,000-cal diet with 1 English muffin in place of crackers	same as for 1,200-cal diet
Calories: 223	290	290

Lunch

1,000 Calories	1,200 Calories	1,400 Calories
½ cup Chicken Salad* made with 1 tbsp imitation mayonnaise 2 oz whole wheat pita pocket bread 8 oz skim milk	same as for 1,000-cal diet with low-fat (1%) instead of skim milk	same as for 1,200-cal diet with 1 cup chicken noodle soup
Calories: 382	412	487

Supper

1,000 Calories	1,200 Calories	1,400 Calories
1 serving Flounder Florentine* 1 medium baked potato ½ cup cooked peas 1 tbsp sour cream 8 oz skim milk	same as for 1,000-cal diet with 1 additional tbsp sour cream, 8 oz low-fat (1%) milk instead of skim	same as for 1,200-cal with 1 additional serving of flounder
Calories: 444	497	637
Totals: 1,049	1,199	1,414

DAY 12

1,000 Calories	1,200 Calories	1,400 Calories

Breakfast

1,000 Calories	1,200 Calories	1,400 Calories
½ banana 1 cup Wheaties 4 oz skimmed milk	½ banana ⅔ cup Wheaties 4 oz low-fat (1%) milk 1 slice toast 1 tsp margarine	same as for 1,200-cal diet
Calories: 200	285	285

Lunch

1,000 Calories	1,200 Calories	1,400 Calories

crisp-cooked or steamed vegetables:
  ⅔ cup broccoli,
  ½ cup carrots,
  1 cup cauliflower
2 oz part-skim mozzarella cheese melted on top
1 English muffin
1 tsp margarine
	same as for 1,000-cal diet	same as for 1,000-cal diet with 8 oz low-low-fat (1%) milk

Calories: 386	386	496

Supper

1,000 Calories	1,200 Calories	1,400 Calories
1 serving Beef Stew* ½ piece Corn Bread*	1 serving Beef Stew* 1 piece Corn Bread*	1 serving Beef Stew* 1 piece Corn Bread* 2 tsp margarine
Calories: 454	564	632
Total: 1,040	1,235	1413

DAY 13

1,000 Calories	1,200 Calories	1,400 Calories

Breakfast

1,000 Calories	1,200 Calories	1,400 Calories
1 tbsp raisins	1 tbsp raisins	same as for 1,200-cal
½ small banana	½ small banana	diet
½ cup cooked oat-	¾ cup cooked oat-	
meal	meal	
8 oz skimmed milk	8 oz low-fat (1%) milk	
Calories: 206	299	299

Lunch

1,000 Calories	1,200 Calories	1,400 Calories
8 oz skimmed milk	same as for 1,000-cal	same as for 1,200-cal
2 slices whole wheat	diet except for 8 oz	diet with 1 cup onion
bread	low-fat (1%) milk	soup
½ cup tuna (3 oz,		
water-packed)		
mixed with		
chopped celery,		
onions, 1 tbsp		
diet mayonnaise		
1 medium apple		
Calories: 403	433	490

Supper

1,000 Calories	1,200 Calories	1,400 Calories
1 serving Chicken	same as for 1,000-cal	same as for 1,200-cal
Cacciatore*	diet with additional	diet with large
½ cup spaghetti	½ cup spaghetti	salad plus 1 tbsp
3 tbsp Parmesan		Italian dressing
cheese		
¼ cup low-salt		
tomato sauce		
⅔ cup broccoli		
1 tsp margarine		
Calories: 416	493	598
Total: 1,025	1,225	1,387

DAY 14

1,000 Calories	1,200 Calories	1,400 Calories

Breakfast

2 Whole Wheat Pancakes* 1 tbsp maple syrup	½ grapefruit Whole-Wheat Pancakes* 1 tbsp maple syrup 1 tbsp apple butter	same as for 1,200-cal diet
Calories: 210	283	283

Lunch

1 serving Chickpea Spread* 2 oz pita pocket bread with raw, chopped vegetables: cucumber, onion, alfalfa sprouts, lettuce 8 oz skimmed milk	same as for 1,000-cal diet except for 8 oz low-fat (1%) milk	same as for 1,200-cal diet with 1 additional serving of chickpea spread
Calories: 349	379	478

Supper

1 serving Baked Sole with Shrimp and Asparagus* ⅔ cup cooked rice large green salad 1 tsp oil plus vinegar as desired 8 oz skimmed milk	same as for 1,000-cal diet except for 8 oz low-fat (1%) milk instead of skimmed milk	same as for 1,200-cal diet with 1 small dinner roll + 1 tsp margarine
Calories: 471	516	635
Total: 1,030	1,178	1,396

DAY 15

1,000 Calories	1,200 Calories	1,400 Calories

Breakfast

1,000 Calories	1,200 Calories	1,400 Calories
2 prunes ½ cup cooked oatmeal 1 slice toast 1 tsp margarine	3 prunes ¾ cup cooked oatmeal 1 slice toast broiled with ¼ cup skim ricotta cheese and dash of cinnamon	same as for 1,200-cal diet
Calories: 208	310	310

Lunch

1,000 Calories	1,200 Calories	1,400 Calories
2 slices of pizza, 14″ diameter 1 cup salad: lettuce, tomato, cucumbers green pepper 1 tbsp Italian dressing	same as for 1,000-cal diet	same as for 1,000-cal diet with 1 oz grated cheese added to salad
Calories: 416	416	516

Supper

1,000 Calories	1,200 Calories	1,400 Calories
1 serving Spicy Baked Fish* ⅔ cup okra ½ cup butternut squash 2 tsp margarine 8 oz skimmed milk ⅔ cup water-packed fruit coctail	same as for 1,000-cal diet except for 2 servings of fish, 8 oz low-fat (1%) milk instead of skimmed	same as for 1,200-cal diet with additional 4 oz low-fat (1%) milk
Calories: 404	544	599
Total: 1,028	1,270	1,425

DAY 16

1,000 Calories	1,200 Calories	1,400 Calories

Breakfast

1,000 Calories	1,200 Calories	1,400 Calories
4 oz orange juice or 1 orange ½ whole-wheat bagel ½ tbsp cream cheese 1 cup sugar-free Alba hot cocoa	4 oz orange juice or 1 orange 1 whole-wheat bagel 1 tbsp cream cheese 1 cup sugar-free Alba hot cocoa	same as for 1,200-cal diet
Calories: 210	310	310

Lunch

1,000 Calories	1,200 Calories	1,400 Calories
2 slices whole-wheat bread 2 oz lean roast beef 2 squares graham crackers	2 slices whole-wheat bread 2 oz lean roast beef 5 Arrowroot cookies	same as for 1,200-cal diet with 1 medium apple
Calories: 322	391	472

Supper

1,000 Calories	1,200 Calories	1,400 Calories
2 Bean and Cheese Enchiladas* green salad 2 tbsp Kraft Zesty reduced-calorie dressing	2 Bean and Cheese Enchiladas* green salad 1 tbsp Italian dressing	same as for 1,200-cal diet with ⅛ honeydew melon
Calories: 509	557	617
Total: 1,041	1,258	1,399

DAY 17

1,000 Calories   *1,200 Calories*   *1,400 Calories*

Breakfast

1,000 Calories	1,200 Calories	1,400 Calories
1 cup plain low-fat yogurt 2 tbsp wheat germ sugar substitute to taste	1 cup low-fat flavored yogurt: vanilla, lemon, or coffee 1 tbsp sunflower seeds 2 tbsp wheat germ	same as for 1,200-cal diet
Calories: 215	296	296

Lunch

1,000 Calories	1,200 Calories	1,400 Calories
2 slices whole-wheat bread 2 oz Swiss cheese 1 medium apple	same as for 1,000-cal diet	same as for 1,000-cal diet plus 3 squares graham crackers
Calories: 427	427	495

Supper

1,000 Calories	1,200 Calories	1,400 Calories
2 Beef Tacos* green salad 1 tsp oil and vinegar dressing	2 Beef Tacos* green salad with 1 tbsp Italian dressing 1 cup melon balls: honeydew or cantaloupe	same as for 1,200-cal diet with 1 additional taco
Calories: 405	480	650
Total: *1,047*	*1,203*	*1,441*

DAY 18

1,000 Calories	1,200 Calories	1,400 Calories

Breakfast

1,000 Calories	1,200 Calories	1,400 Calories
4 oz orange juice or 1 orange 1 scrambled egg made with Pam 1 slice whole-wheat toast 1 tsp preserves	4 oz orange juice or 1 orange 1 scrambled egg made with Pam 2 slices whole-wheat toast 2 tsp preserves	same as for 1,200-cal diet
Calories: 212	294	294

Lunch

1,000 Calories	1,200 Calories	1,400 Calories
1 cup cooked spaghetti with 1/4 cup low-salt tomato sauce 3 tbsp Parmesan cheese green salad 1 tsp corn oil and vinegar dressing 8 oz skim milk	same as for 1,000-cal diet with 8 oz low-fat (1%) milk instead of skimmed milk	same as for 1,200-cal diet with 1 small dinner roll
Calories: 424	454	539

Supper

1,000 Calories	1,200 Calories	1,400 Calories
4 oz broiled scallops tossed with 1 tsp oil plus 1 tsp lemon juice before broiling 1 medium baked potato ½ cup carrots ⅔ cup blueberries	6 oz broiled scallops prepared as with 1,000-cal diet 2 tbsp sour cream with potato	same as for 1,200-cal diet with green salad plus 1 tbsp Italian dressing
Calories: 397	506	591
Total: 1,033	1,254	1,424

DAY 19

1,000 Calories	1,200 Calories	1,400 Calories

Breakfast

1 tbsp raisins ½ cup spoon-size shredded wheat 8 oz skimmed milk	2 tbsp raisins 1 cup spoon-size shredded wheat 8 oz low-fat (1%) milk	same as for 1,200-cal diet
Calories: 178	306	306

Lunch

2 Beef Tacos* green salad 1 tsp oil and vinegar dressing	same as for 1,000-cal diet	same as for 1,000-cal diet with 1 cup fresh fruit salad
Calories: 405	405	479

Supper

1 serving Linguini with Clam Sauce* 3 tbsp Parmesan cheese ⅔ cup broccoli 1 small dinner roll 2 tsp margarine	same as for 1,000-cal diet with 8 oz low-fat (1%) milk	same as for 1,200-cal diet with 1 cup Vegetable Chowder*
Calories: 423	533	658
Total: 1,006	1,244	1,443

DAY 20

1,000 Calories	1,200 Calories	1,400 Calories

Breakfast

1,000 Calories	1,200 Calories	1,400 Calories
½ cup strawberries: fresh or frozen, no added sugar ½ cup plain low-fat yogurt 1 packet sugar substitute ½ bran muffin (1½ oz)	1 cup strawberries: fresh or frozen, no added sugar 1 cup plain low-fat yogurt 1 packet sugar substitute ½ bran muffin (1½ oz)	same as for 1,200-cal diet
Calories: 208	313	313

Lunch

1,000 Calories	1,200 Calories	1,400 Calories
2 oz pita pocket bread stuffed with 3 oz chicken, (no skin) diced celery, onions, green pepper 1 tsp imitation mayonnaise 1 cup Alba sugar-free hot cocoa	same as for 1,000-cal diet	same as for 1,000-cal diet with 1 medium apple
Calories: 415	415	496

Supper

1,000 Calories	1,200 Calories	1,400 Calories
1 serving Fiesta Fish* ⅔ cup rice ½ cup carrots	same as for 1,000-cal diet with 1 small dinner roll, 1 tsp margarine	same as for 1,200-cal diet with 8 oz low-fat (1%) milk
Calories: 396	515	625
Total: 1,019	1,243	1,434

DAY 21

1,000 Calories   *1,200 Calories*   *1,400 Calories*

Breakfast

4 oz orange juice or 1 orange 1 whole-wheat English muffin ¼ cup low-fat (1%) cottage cheese	4 oz orange juice or 1 orange 1 whole-wheat English muffin with 1 oz Swiss cheese melted on top	same as for 1,200-cal diet

Calories: 217   292   292

Lunch

2 tbsp peanut butter 3 triple Rye-Krisp crackers 1 cup cut-up vegetables	2 tbsp peanut butter 2 slices whole-wheat bread 1 tbsp jam or jelly 1 cup cut-up vegetables	same as for 1,200-cal diet with sliced banana added to sandwich

Calories: 288   402   507

Supper

1 serving Quiche* green salad 1 tbsp Italian dressing Oatmeal Muffin* 8 oz skimmed milk	1 serving Quiche* green salad 1 tbsp Italian dressing Oatmeal Muffin* 8 oz low-fat (1%) milk	same as for 1,200-cal diet plus 1 tsp margarine and additional 4 oz low-fat (1%) milk

Calories: 522   552   641

Total: *1,027*   *1,246*   *1,440*

C/SCHOOL LUNCHES AND SNACKS

Recipes for items marked with an asterisk (*) are provided in Appendix E unless otherwise indicated.

DAY 1

8 oz of milk (low-fat or skim)
2 slices of rye bread
2 servings of Chickpea Spread*
1 apple   531 calories

DAY 2

8 oz of milk (low-fat or skim)
2 Beef Tacos*
1 small orange   510 calories

DAY 3

8 oz of milk (low-fat or skim)
2 slices of whole-wheat bread
2 oz of low-fat turkey meat
1-2 pieces of lettuce
1 pear   500 calories

DAY 4

8 oz of milk (low-fat or skim)
2 slices of pumpernickel bread
½ cup Chicken Salad*
3 graham cracker squares   500 calories

DAY 5

8 oz of milk (low-fat or skim)
2 slices of whole-wheat bread
2 tbsp peanut butter
1 banana sliced on top of peanut
   butter sandwiches
carrot and celery sticks   550 calories

DAY 6

8 oz of milk (low-fat or skim)
1 hamburger (2 oz lean ground beef)
1 hamburger roll
1 tangerine   550 calories

DAY 7

8 oz of milk (low-fat or skim)
½ cup Tuna-Apple Salad*
1 Oatmeal Muffin*   518 calories

SNACKS

1. 1 bagel with 1 tbsp cream cheese or 4 tsp cheese spread
2. 1 frozen fruit and juice bar

3. 1 plain, raisin, or peanut butter granola bar
4. 1 corn, bran, or Oatmeal Muffin*
5. 1 apple with 1 oz Cheddar cheese
6. 2½ oz pistachio nuts roasted in shell
7. 1 oz peanuts with 2 tbsp raisins
8. 8 oz of low-fat or skim milk with 1¼ cup Cheerios, 1 cup of Wheaties, 1 cup of Corn Chex, ⅔ cup of Wheat Chex, 3 graham cracker squares, or 8 Nabisco Wheatsworth stone-ground wheat crackers.
9. 1 stalk of celery with 1 tbsp peanut butter
10. 1 oz pretzels
11. nachos: place 1½ oz of Cheddar cheese and 1 tbsp tomato sauce on tortilla; melt under broiler oven
12. grilled cheese sandwich: broil 1 slice (1 oz) of cheese on 1 slice of whole-wheat bread or ½ English muffin
13. Chili Bean Dip* and raw vegetables (carrots, celery, green peppers) or whole-wheat crackers
14. Nature Crunch* (see Appendix D)
15. Back-Packer's Mix* (see Appendix D)
16. Yogurt Fruit Crunch*
17. **Popcorn:** 2 to 4 cups (with ½ tbsp margarine, if desired)

D/POPCORN RECIPES

The recipes in this appendix have been selected from *Popcorn* by Larry Kusche, © HPBooks, Inc., Box 5367, Tucson, AZ 85703. (602) 888-2150.

In keeping with the principles of the Popcorn-*Plus* Diet, those recipes marked with an asterisk (*) have been modified slightly by (1) substituting margarine or Butter Buds for butter, (2) using ½ to ¾ less sugar and salt than called for in the original recipes, and (3) using low-fat or skim milk.

BREAKFAST

Toasted Popcorn Flakes*

1 quart popped popcorn
  (4 cups)
1 tbsp margarine or Butter
  Buds

2 to 3 cups low-fat or skim
  milk

1. Preheat oven to 400 degrees F.
2. Melt margarine over low heat (or substitute Butter Buds). Drizzle over the popcorn.
3. Place in the oven on a cookie sheet until crisp and slightly brown, approximately 5 min.
4. Pour into cereal bowls. Add milk and fresh fruit as desired.

Makes 4 servings, 100 to 140 calories per serving.

Honey-Frosted Flakes*

1 quart popped popcorn (4 cups)	¼ cup raisins
¼ cup honey	2 cups low-fat or skim milk

1. Preheat oven to 250 degrees F. Lightly oil a cookie sheet.
2. Mix popcorn and raisins together and spread in a large, oiled baking pan 4" deep. Keep warm in oven.
3. Boil honey for several minutes, being careful not to let it burn.
4. Remove popcorn from oven.
5. While honey is still foamy, pour it over popcorn and raisins, mixing thoroughly.
6. Spread out on cookie sheet and separate into individual pieces, if possible.
7. After completely cool, store in a covered container.
8. Use like any other dry cereal, adding milk and fruit as desired.

Makes 4 to 6 servings, 160 to 175 calories per serving.

LUNCH OR SUPPER

Several of the following recipes involve ground, popped popcorn. For finely ground popcorn, put a handful of *popped* popcorn into your blender or food processor. Turn it on *low* for a minute or two. Add a handful at a time to make more. Two cups of popped popcorn will make about one cup of finely ground popcorn. For medium-ground, grind it for around 20 seconds.

Pop 'N Bake Chicken*

½ to 1 cup finely ground, popped popcorn	1 tsp paprika
1 broiler-fryer chicken, cut up (around 2½ lbs.)	¼ tsp pepper
½ tsp salt	¼ cup vegetable oil

1. Preheat oven to 400 degrees F.
2. Wash chicken and pat dry.
3. Mix together ground popcorn, salt, paprika, and pepper.
4. Coat chicken with popcorn mixture (3).
5. Pour oil into shallow baking pan.
6. Arrange chicken skin-side down in oil. Bake for 30 min.
7. Turn chicken. Bake 30 minutes more or until tender.

Variation: add 1/4 tsp garlic powder and 1/2 tsp crushed tarragon to coating mix.

Makes 6 servings, 230 calories per serving.

Stuffed Peppers

1 cup finely ground, popped popcorn
3 large green peppers
3 to 4 cups boiling, salted water
¾ lb lean ground beef
2 tbsp finely chopped onions

2 tbsp finely chopped onions
½ tsp salt
1 tsp Worcestershire sauce
¼ tsp pepper
8 oz can of tomato sauce

1. Preheat oven to 350 degrees F. Cut peppers in half. Remove seeds.
2. Cook for 5 minutes in boiling, salted water.
3. Drain. Then mix other ingredients together and fill peppers.
4. Bake in a covered casserole for one hour.
5. Uncover and continue baking for 15 minutes.

Makes 6 servings, 140 calories per serving.

Potato Casserole*

2½ cups finely ground, popped popcorn
2 cups hot mashed potatoes (3 or 4 medium-sized)
1 tsp finely chopped onion
1 tbsp chopped fresh parsley

2 tbsp margarine or Butter Buds
1 cup low-fat cottage cheese
½ cup grated cheddar cheese

1. Preheat oven to 350 degrees F. Oil a one-quart casserole.
2. Mix together hot mashed potatoes, onion, parsley, margarine (or Butter Buds), ground popcorn, and cottage cheese.
3. Spread in casserole. Sprinkle with cheddar cheese.
4. Cover. Bake for 20 minutes.

Makes 6 servings, 150-180 calories per serving.

Garlic Croutons*

1 quart popped popcorn (4 cups)   2 tbsp butter, margarine (or
1 garlic clove   substitute Butter Buds).

1. In a small skillet, melt butter, margarine, or Butter Buds over low heat.
2. Chop garlic. Add to melting butter, margarine, or Butter Buds.
3. Simmer over low heat for 3 to 5 min.
4. Remove garlic pieces.
5. Drizzle butter, margarine, or Butter Buds over popcorn.
6. Store leftover croutons in an airtight container for several days.

Makes 1 quart.

DESSERTS

Popcorn Balls*

You are about to embark on one of the all-time great popcorn delights—popcorn balls. They're terrific for Halloween, birthday parties, and as gifts for any number of occasions. Don't give them all away, though. Save some for yourself. Keep in mind that they're *desserts*—150 to 200 calories apiece. So enjoy them thoughtfully.

Making popcorn balls is a wonderful family project. The first time through might be a little slow. But you'll soon get the hang of it. As you tackle the recipe, remember: when all else fails, *follow the instructions!*

First, get out all the ingredients, measuring cups, and pans. Keeping the popcorn warm in the oven before you add the syrup will prevent the liquid from hardening as it touches the mixing pan. Keep all surfaces that the syrup will touch lightly oiled to prevent sticking. Wear rubber gloves to keep your hands from getting burned.

In forming the balls, press the popcorn gently into shape. This makes for less dense, easier-to-eat balls. You may need to pack them several times as they cool. Make sure to remove any unpopped kernels before making the balls. This can prevent some unpleasant, tooth-breaking surprises.

Add variety to your popcorn balls by mixing in one or two cups of whole or chopped nuts. You can also enclose foil-wrapped fortunes.

2 quarts popped popcorn (8 cups)
⅔ cup sugar (or less)
⅓ cup light corn syrup
⅓ cup water
¼ cup (4 tbsp) margarine or Butter Buds
⅛ tsp salt
1 tsp vanilla

1. Preheat oven to 250 degrees F. Put popcorn in large baking pan at least 4″ deep. Keep warm in the oven.
2. Combine sugar, corn syrup, water, margarine (or Butter Buds) and salt in large saucepan. Stir over medium heat until sugar is dissolved.
3. Cook until mixture reaches 250 degrees F on a candy thermometer, stirring frequently.
4. Remove from heat. Stir in vanilla.
5. Remove popcorn from oven. Pour syrup mixture over popcorn, stirring to mix well.
6. Using lightly oiled gloves, form into balls.

Makes 8 balls, 150 to 200 calories per serving.

Popcorn Brittle*

1 quart popped popcorn (4 cups)	2 tbsp water (1 oz)
1 cup margarine or Butter Buds	1 tbsp light corn syrup
1 cup sugar	½ cup granola

1. Cut a large sheet of waxed paper to fit a cooky sheet. Lightly oil the waxed paper.
2. Melt margarine (or heat Butter Buds) in a 3-quart saucepan over low heat.
3. Remove from heat and blend in sugar.
4. Return to low heat, stirring constantly, until mixture reaches full boil.
5. Stir in water and corn syrup.
6. Continue stirring over low heat until mixture reaches 270 degrees F on a candy thermometer
7. Remove from heat. Stir in popcorn and granola.
8. Cool until hardened. Break into 8 to 12 large pieces.

Makes approximately one quart, 150 to 200 calories per serving.

SNACKS

Back-Packer's Mix

3 quarts popped popcorn	1 cup shredded fresh coconut
1 cup peanuts	1 cup sunflower seeds
1 cup raisins	¼ tsp salt, if desired

1. Make sure the popcorn is cool.
2. Mix all ingredients well.
3. Pack loosely in empty coffee cans with plastic covers or in plastic sandwich bags.

Makes 3 to 4 quarts, 150 to 180 calories per 3 oz. serving.

Nature Crunch*

2 quarts popped popcorn
1 cup peanuts
1 cup wheat germ
1 cup raisins
¼ cup margarine

¼ cup sugar
⅓ cup honey
⅔ cup water
½ tsp salt

1. Preheat oven to 250 degrees F. Mix popcorn, peanuts, and wheat germ in a large, 4"-deep oiled baking pan. Keep warm in oven.
2. Oil two large 2" deep baking pans.
3. In a large saucepan, melt margarine. Stir in sugar, honey, water, and salt.
4. Cook over medium heat, stirring constantly, until sugar is dissolved and mixture starts to boil. Cook until mixture reaches 250 degrees F on a candy thermometer.
5. Remove popcorn mixture (1) from oven. Stir in raisins.
6. Pour syrup mixture slowly over popcorn mixture, stirring to coat.
7. Spread 1" deep in oiled baking pans. Bake 45 min., stirring occasionally.
8. Cool. Break or cut apart.

Makes 3 quarts, 150 calories per 3 oz. serving.

E/OTHER RECIPES

These recipes supplement Appendix B. They can be used both with the maintenance as well as the weight-loss phases of the Popcorn-*Plus* Diet.

Baked Fish With Creole Sauce

¾ lb fresh or frozen fillets or 1½ lbs whole fish
½ small onion, chopped
⅓ small green pepper, thinly sliced

8 oz can tomato sauce
1 tsp chili powder
¼ tsp salt
⅛ tsp pepper

1. Thaw fish, if frozen.
2. Rinse fish in cool water. Drain well.
3. Preheat oven to 350 degrees F.
4. Place fish in 2" deep baking pan.
5. Mix together onion, green pepper, tomato sauce, chili powder, salt, and pepper. Pour over fish.
6. Cover pan and bake until fish flakes easily with fork (20 to 30 min. for fillets, 30 to 40 min. for whole fish).

   Makes 4 servings, 91 calories per serving.

Baked Mini-Meat Loaf

¾ lb lean ground beef, or
¼ lb lean ground pork and
½ lb lean ground beef
¾ cup uncooked oatmeal

¼ cup onion, grated
¼ tsp salt
⅛ tsp pepper

1. Mix all ingredients together.
2. Form into four loaves about 2" high.
3. Place in large ungreased baking pan.
4. Bake at 375 degrees F until brown and cooked through, about 25 to 30 min.
5. Pour fat from pan before serving.

Makes 4 servings, 275 calories per serving.

Baked Sole with Shrimp and Asparagus*

4 sole filets (3 oz each)
4 large uncooked shrimp
4 asparagus tips, steamed to
    crisp tender

fresh dill springs (or dried dill
    weed)
fresh lemon juice
paprika

1. Preheat oven to 350 degrees F.
2. Shell and clean shrimp.
3. Place 1 shrimp in center of each sole filet.
4. Put an asparagus tip on top of each shrimp and form a roll with sole filet. Secure with toothpick, if needed.
5. Place fish rolls in baking dish.
6. Squeeze lemon juice over filets. Sprinkle with dill and paprika.
7. Bake for 20 min. or until fish flakes.

Makes 4 servings, 170 calories per serving.

Bean and Cheese Enchiladas

8 large corn tortillas
1 tsp oil
1 green pepper, chopped
2 small onions, chopped
3 tbsp chili powder
¾ tsp garlic powder
¾ tsp onion powder

1⅔ cups cooked kidney beans
½ cup low-fat cottage cheese
10¾ oz can tomato puree or
    sauce
2 oz grated Monterey Jack
    cheese

1. Cook onions and green pepper in oil until soft.
2. Drain beans and mash.
3. Add together and mix well 2 tbsp of chili powder, ½ tsp of garlic powder, 3 tbsp of tomato puree or sauce, cottage cheese, onions, and green pepper to the mashed beans.
4. Place 3 tbsp of the bean and cheese mixture from step 3 on each tortilla.
5. Roll tortillas and place in baking dish.
6. Combine remainder of tomato puree and garlic powder with ¾ tspn onion powder in a small bowl. Stir well.
7. Pour the sauce from step 6 over the enchiladas. Top with grated cheese.
8. Cover and bake at 350 degrees F for 20 to 30 mins., until heated through and cheese on top is melted.
    Variations: Red pepper, cayenne pepper, or tabasco sauce may be added to filling and/or sauce.

Makes 4 servings, 472 calories per serving.

Beef, Beans, and Macaroni Chili

½ lb ground beef
1 small onion, chopped
2 cups canned tomatoes
    (save liquid)
1¾ cups cooked kidney beans
    (save liquid)

2 tsp chili powder
¾ cup uncooked elbow
    macaroni

1. Fry ground beef and onions in pan until lightly browned. Drain off fat.

2. Chop tomatoes.
3. Add enough water to tomato and bean liquid to equal 1 cup.
4. Add chopped tomatoes, kidney beans, liquid from step 3, chili powder, and macaroni to beef mixture.
5. Simmer, covered, about 20 min. until macaroni is tender. Stir occasionally to keep from sticking.
6. Thin with a little water, as necessary, during cooking.
   Variations: Add red pepper, cayenne pepper, or tabasco sauce for more spice.

Makes 4 servings, 1 cup each, 333 calories per serving.

Beef With Chinese-Style Vegetables

1 lb lean beef round steak, boneless
⅔ cup green beans, cut into strips
⅔ cup carrots, thinly sliced
⅔ cup turnips, thinly sliced
⅔ cup cauliflower florets, thinly sliced
⅔ cup Chinese cabbage, cut into strips

⅔ cup boiling water
2 tsp oil
4 tsp cornstarch
½ tsp ground ginger
⅛ tsp garlic powder
1 tbsp soy sauce
3 tbsp sherry (or water)
½ cup water

1. Trim fat from beef. Slice across grain into thin strips, ⅛" by 3".
2. Add vegetables to boiling water. Simmer, covered, for 5 min. or until vegetables are tender but still crisp. Drain.
3. While vegetables are cooking, heat oil in nonstick frying pan. Add beef and stir-fry over moderate heat, turning pieces constantly until beef is no longer red, about 2 to 3 min.
4. Mix cornstarch, garlic powder, ginger, soy sauce, sherry (or water), and water.
5. Stir cornstarch mixture from step 4 into beef. Heat until sauce starts to boil.
6. Serve meat sauce over vegetables.

Makes 4 servings (½ cup of meat, ½ cup of vegetables), 200 calories per serving (185 if made without sherry).

Beef Stew

½ lb beef, chuck (lean)
2 medium onions, cubed
4 medium potatoes, cubed
10 oz package of frozen mixed
   vegetables

1 tsp oil
2 tbsp white flour
3¼ cups water
dash pepper
¼ tsp garlic powder

1. Cut beef into cubes. Brown on all sides in oil.
2. Add 3 cups water and simmer ¾ hour.
3. Add onions and potatoes. Simmer ½ hour longer.
4. Add pepper, garlic powder, and frozen mixed vegetables. Cook another 10 min. or until potatoes are done.
5. Make a paste with remaining ¼ cup water and 2 tbsp flour. Add paste to stew while stirring.
6. Cook stew about 3 min. more until thickened. Add water if stew becomes too thick.

Makes 4 servings, 1¼ cups each, 344 calories per serving.

Beef Tacos

12 taco shells, fully cooked
1 lb lean ground beef
¼ cup chopped onion
8 oz canned tomato sauce

2 tsp chili powder
1 cup chopped tomato
1 cup shredded lettuce
½ cup (2 oz) natural sharp
   Cheddar cheese

1. Brown ground beef and onion in frying pan. Drain excess fat.
2. Stir in tomato sauce and chili powder. Bring to a boil.
3. Reduce heat. Cook 10 to 15 min. uncovered, stirring occasionally until mixture is dry and crumbly.
4. Fill taco shells with approximately 2 tbsp of meat mixture.
5. Mix tomato, lettuce, and cheese.
6. Spoon about 2 tbsp over beef into taco shells.

Makes 6 servings, 2 tacos each, 340 calories per serving.

Chicken Cacciatore

1 small onion, chopped
¼ cup water
1 cup canned tomatoes
½ cup tomato puree or sauce

½ tsp garlic powder
1 tsp oregano
⅛ tsp pepper
4 chicken pieces (3 to 4 oz each)

1. Boil onion in water until tender in a covered 1-qt. saucepan. Do not drain.
2. Add tomatoes, tomato puree (or sauce), garlic powder, oregano, and pepper to onions. Simmer 10 min. to blend flavors.
3. Place chicken in frying pan. Pour tomato mixture over chicken.
4. Cook, covered, over low heat until chicken is tender, about 45 min.
5. Uncover and cook 15 more min. to thicken tomato sauce.

Makes 4 servings, 1 piece of chicken each, around 220 calories per serving.

Chicken Salad

½ chicken (8 oz)
2 large stalks celery, chopped
¾ cup apple chunks

2 tbsp diet mayonnaise
¼ tsp salt

1. Boil chicken in water. Simmer until tender (45 to 60 min.)
2. Cool, remove skin and bone. Chop coarsely into ½" pieces.
3. Mix all ingredients together.

Makes 4 servings, ½ cup each, 150 calories per serving.

Chickpea Spread

1¾ cups cooked chickpeas or garbanzo beans (save liquid)
2 tbsp lemon juice

1 tbsp mayonnaise
¼ tsp garlic powder

1. Drain chickpeas, saving liquid.
2. Mash and blend chickpeas. Add 1 tbsp chickpea liquid to the lemon juice, mayonnaise, and garlic powder. Mix until smooth.
3. If too thick, add a little more chickpea liquid or water.
   Variation: Instead of canned beans, you can use dry beans and cook them. To cook dry beans, cover with 2 to 3 times as much water as beans. Soak overnight, add water, and cook 1½ to 2 hours.

Makes 6 servings, 100 calories per serving.

Chili Bean Dip

16 oz canned kidney beans, drained
1 tbsp vinegar
¾ tsp chili powder

⅛ tsp ground cumin
2 tsp finely chopped onion
2 tsp chopped parsley

1. Place drained beans, vinegar, chili powder, and cumin in blender. Blend until smooth.
2. Remove mixture from blender. Stir in onion and parsley.
3. Serve with raw vegetable sticks.

Makes 1⅔ cups, 15 calories per tbsp.

Corn Bread

2 cups stone-ground (or degerminated) cornmeal
1 tbsp baking powder
¼ tsp salt
1 egg, slightly beaten

1 cup milk
2 tbsp honey
¼ cup oil

1. Preheat oven to 400 degrees F.
2. Grease an 8x8x2-inch baking pan.
3. Mix cornmeal, baking powder, and salt thoroughly.

4. Mix egg, milk, honey, and oil. Add to cornmeal mixture.
5. Stir only until dry ingredients are moistened. Batter will be lumpy.
6. Pour into pan.
7. Bake 20 min. or until lightly browned.

Makes 8 servings, 2 by 4 inches each, 220 calories per serving.

Fiesta Fish*

2 lbs. fresh white fish
1 cup chopped tomatoes
1 whole green pepper, chopped
2 tbsp fresh red onion, chopped
3 tbsp lemon juice

1 tbsp olive oil
1 tsp dried basil
½ tsp freshly ground black pepper
¼ tsp chili powder

1. Preheat oven to 350 degrees F.
2. Mix lemon juice, basil, pepper, and chili powder. Set aside.
3. Heat olive oil in skillet and saute green pepper, onion, and tomatoes 1-2 mins. to soften. Then remove from heat.
4. Place fish in baking dish. Cover with mixture from step 2.
5. Pour lemon juice mixture (step 2) over fish.
6. Cover baking dish with aluminum foil and bake 25 to 30 min. until fish is tender and flakes with a fork.

Makes 6 servings, 235 calories per serving.

Flounder Florentine

1 lb frozen skinless flounder fillets, thawed
1½ cups boiling water
10 oz package of frozen chopped spinach
1 tbsp onion, finely chopped
½ tsp marjoram

2 tbsp flour
1 cup skim milk
½ tsp salt
2 tbsp grated Parmesan cheese
dash of pepper

1. Place fish fillets in cup boiling water. Cook, uncovered, 2 min. Drain.
2. Place spinach and onion in ½ cup boiling water. Separate spinach with fork.
3. When water returns to boiling, cover and cook spinach 2 min. Drain well. Mix with marjoram.
4. Put spinach in 8x8x2-inch glass baking dish. Arrange cooked fish on top of spinach.
5. Mix flour thoroughly with ¼ cup of milk.
6. Pour remaining milk into saucepan. Heat.
7. Add flour mixture slowly to hot milk, stirring constantly. Cook, stirring constantly, until thickened.
8. Stir in salt and pepper.
9. Pour sauce over fish. Sprinkle with Parmesan cheese.
10. Bake at 400 degrees F until top is lightly browned and mixture is bubbly (around 25 min.).

Makes 4 servings, 3 oz fish and ¼ cup spinach each, 140 calories per serving.

Linguini with Clam Sauce*

1 lb fresh (or canned, peeled) whole tomatoes
10 oz can cooked clams
1 clove fresh garlic
2 tbsp capers

3 tbsp fresh parsley, chopped
1 tsp olive oil
½ tsp freshly ground black pepper
½ lb cooked and drained pasta

1. Poach tomatoes in boiling water or steam until tender (5 to 10 min.).
2. Peel and chop tomatoes, saving liquid.
3. Heat olive oil in large, nonstick skillet or cast-iron pan.
4. Saute garlic and capers 1 min. Add parsley and tomatoes with liquid saved from step 2.
5. Reduce heat and simmer 5 min.
6. Sprinkle in pepper and stir.
7. Drain clams, saving ½ cup liquid.

8. Add clams and liquid from step 7 to mixture. Simmer 1 to 2 min. until clams are heated through.
9. Serve over pasta.

Makes 4 servings, 150 calories per serving.

Oatmeal Muffins

¾ cup whole wheat flour
¾ cup white flour
1 cup uncooked oatmeal
1 tbsp baking powder
3 tbsp sugar

¼ tsp salt
1 egg
1 cup low-fat (1%) milk
¼ cup oil

1. Preheat oven to 400 degrees F.
2. Combine flours, oatmeal, baking powder, sugar, and salt. Mix well.
3. In a separate bowl, beat egg. Add milk and oil. Stir well.
4. Add liquid mixture (3) to flour mixture (2). Stir until just blended. Batter should be a little lumpy.
5. Pour into greased and floured muffin pan.
6. Bake 15 to 20 min. or until muffins spring back when touched.

Makes 12 muffins, 150 calories per muffin.

Quiche*

¼ to ½ cup chicken broth
½ tsp garlic, minced
2 medium zucchini, shredded
    and well drained
2 tbsp grated Parmesan cheese
½ lb broccoli, chopped and
    steamed
1¼ cup nonfat milk

3 oz low-fat cheese, shredded
3 tbsp nonfat dry milk powder
2 whole eggs, separated
1 egg white
2 tbsp tomato paste
1 tbsp dried basil leaves,
    crushed
dash of red pepper

1. Preheat oven to 350 degrees F.
2. Heat 3 to 4 tbsp of chicken broth in nonstick skillet.
3. When reduced and browned, add minced garlic and saute for 1 min.
4. Add zucchini and cook about 3 min.
5. Add 1 tbsp Parmesan cheese and cook 1 more min.
6. Put mixture on bottom of 8-inch quiche pan and spread thinly as for a crust.
7. Arrange broccoli on top. Sprinkle with shredded low-fat cheese.
8. Mix dry milk with nonfat milk until dissolved.
9. Add egg yolks and mix well.
10. Add tomato paste, basil leaves, and red pepper.
11. Beat egg whites until stiff and fold into milk mixture.
12. Pour mixture into zucchini-lined pan.
13. Sprinkle with 1 tbsp Parmesan cheese.
14. Bake 30 min. or until set in the center.

Makes 4 servings, 207 calories per serving.

Spicy Baked Fish

1 lb cod fillets, fresh or frozen, without skin

¼ cup onion, chopped

¼ cup green pepper, chopped

2 tsp oil

8 oz can of whole tomatoes

¼ tsp salt

⅛ tsp pepper

1. Thaw frozen fish.
2. Grease 9x9x2-inch baking pan lightly with ½ tsp oil.
3. Cut fish into 4 pieces. Place in baking pan.
4. Bake at 350 degrees F. until fish flakes easily, about 20 min. Drain cooking liquid from fish.
5. While fish is baking, cook onion and green pepper in remaining oil until onion is clear.
6. Cut up tomatoes into large pieces.

7. Add tomatoes, salt, and pepper to cooked onion and green pepper. Cook 20 min. to blend flavors.
8. Pour sauce over drained fish. Bake 10 min.

Makes 4 servings, about 2½ oz fish each, 110 calories per serving.

Tuna-Apple Salad

6½- or 7-ounce can of tuna fish (packed in water)
1 unpeeled diced apple
1 stalk of celery, chopped

2 tbsp imitation mayonnaise
1 tbsp lemon juice
lettuce as desired

1. Rinse and drain tuna.
2. Mix tuna and other ingredients (except lettuce) in bowl.
3. Use immediately or chill 1 to 2 hours.
4. Serve in sandwich or on bed of lettuce leaves.

Makes 4 servings, ½ cup each, 100 calories per serving.

Vegetable Chowder

2 tbsp onion, chopped
¼ cup celery, chopped
2 tbsp green pepper, chopped

1 tbsp margarine
½ cup potatoes, pared, diced
1 cup water

⅛ tsp marjoram, dried

¼ tsp salt
⅛ tsp pepper
1 cup frozen whole kernel corn
½ cup frozen cut green beans
2 tbsp whole wheat flour
1½ cups whole (or low-fat) milk

1. Cook onion, celery, and green pepper in margarine until almost tender.

2. Add potatoes, water, and seasonings.
3. Cover and simmer until potatoes are tender, about 20 min.
4. Add corn and beans.
5. Cover and simmer 10 min. longer or until beans are tender.
6. Mix flour with small amount of milk. Add to remaining milk.
7. Stir milk mixture into cooked vegetable mixture.
8. Cook, stirring constantly, until slightly thickened.

Makes 4 servings, about 1 cup each, 150 calories per serving (125 calories if made with low-fat milk).

Whole-Wheat Pancakes

¾ cup whole-wheat flour
¾ cup white flour
2½ tsp baking powder
½ tsp salt

½ cup nonfat dry milk
1¼ cups water
1 egg
3 tbsp oil

1. Put dry ingredients into large bowl and mix well.
2. Beat egg. Add water and oil. Beat further until mixed.
3. Mix liquid ingredients into dry ingredients. Stir only until mixed. Batter will be lumpy.
4. Cook on lightly greased hot griddle or pan. Turn over when bubbles appear. Continue cooking until golden brown.
5. Freeze extra pancakes. Heat in toaster before serving.

Makes 16 pancakes, 3½" in diameter, around 100 calories per pancake.

Yogurt Fruit Crunch

2 cups plain low-fat yogurt
1 cup granola or other dry,
  crunchy cereal

1 cup fruit, fresh or canned in
  light syrup or natural juices

1. Spoon layers of cereal, yogurt, and fruit into four individual bowls.

   Makes 4 servings, 1 cup each, 250 calories per cup.

---

*Reprinted with permission from *The Guiltless Gourmet*, Judy Gilliard and Joy Kirkpatrick, Nutrition Wise, Box 499, Rancho Mirage, CA 92270.

Other recipes from *Eating for Better Health* (USDA, Food and Nutrition Service, Program Aid No.1290, Aug. 1981) and *Ideas for Better Eating* (USDA, Science and Education Administration/Human Nutrition, Jan. 1981), Superintendent of Documents, U.S. Government Printing Office, Washington, DC 20402.

F/CALORIC CONTENT OF EVERYDAY FOODS

Beverages	Calories
alcoholic	
beer (8-12 oz)	100-150
whiskey, gin, rum, vodka	
(80-100 proof)	95-125
wines (table, 3½ oz)	85
wines (dessert, 3½ oz)	75-150
colas (8-12 oz)	75-170
fruit juices (8 oz)	
apple	120
cranberry juice cocktail	160
grape juice	170
grapefruit (unsweetened)	100
grapefruit (sweetened)	120
lemonade (pre-sweetened)	110
orange (unsweetened)	120
pineapple (unsweetened)	140
V-8	50
milk (8 oz)	
skim	80-90
low-fat (1%)	110
whole	150

Breads (1 piece)	**Calories**
bagel (plain, 3½″ diameter)	160-200
English muffin	140
muffin (1.4 oz)	
blueberry	110-135
bran	104-125
corn	126-145
pita (6½″ diameter)	165
pumpernickel	80
rye bread	60
white bread	
regular (18 slices/lb)	70
thin (22 slices/lb)	55
whole-wheat bread	60-70

Cereals (1 piece)	**Calories**
bran flakes (1 oz, around 4/5 cup)	85-90
Cheerios (1 oz, around 1¼ cup)	110
corn flakes (1 oz, around 1 1/6 cups)	110
Grape-Nuts (1 oz, around 1/4 cup)	100
Nature Valley Granola (1 oz, about ⅓ cup)	125
oatmeal (cooked, ¾ cup)	100
puffed oats (1 oz, around 1 1/6 cups)	115
puffed rice (1 oz, around 2 cups)	120
puffed wheat (1 oz, around 2 cups)	110
Raisin Bran (1 oz, around ¾ cup)	90
Rice Krispies (1 oz, around 1 cup)	110
shredded wheat (1 oz, 1 large biscuit or ½ cup bitesize)	90-100
Special K (1 oz, around 1⅓ cup)	110
Sugar Frosted Flakes (1 oz, around ¾ cup)	110
Wheaties (1 oz, around 1 cup)	100

Dairy Products (1 piece)	**Calories**
butter (1 pat: 1x⅓″)	35
butter (1 tbsp)	100

cheese (1 oz, or as indicated)

American	105
Cheddar	115
cottage (creamed, 1 cup)	215-235
cottage (creamed, low-fat, 1 cup)	205
cottage (uncreamed, low-fat, 1 cup)	125
cream	100
Parmesan	110-130
Parmesan (grated, 1 tbsp)	25
Swiss	95-105
ice cream (1 cup, vanilla)	270
ice milk (1 cup, vanilla)	185
milk (see **Beverages**)	
yogurt (8 oz, skim milk)	125
yogurt (8 oz, partially skim milk)	150

Fruits (1 piece)	**Calories**
apple (5-8 oz)	80-125
banana (5-7 oz)	85-100
blueberries (½ cup)	45
cantaloupe (½ of 5″ melon)	80
cherries (sweet, 10)	50
dates (3)	66
figs (1 medium)	40
grapefruit (½ of 3¾″ fruit, 8-9 oz)	45-50
grapes (seedless, 10)	34
honeydew melon (2x7″ wedge, 8 oz)	50
orange (2⅝″)	65
peach (4 oz, 2½″)	40
pear (3½x2½″, 6-7 oz)	100
pineapple (raw, 1 cup)	80
raisins (1 cup)	210-240
strawberries (½ cup)	30
tangerine (4 oz)	40
watermelon (4x8″ wedge with rind and seeds)	155

Meat/Poultry (1 piece)	**Calories (cooked)**
beef (3 oz)	
hamburger	185-245

with roll	305-365
with cheese and roll	405-465
Big Mac (McDonald's)	563
Whopper (Burger King)	670
oven roast	160-375
steak	160-350
veal cutlet (trimmed)	185
veal roast	230
bologna (2 slices, 2 oz)	180
braunschweiger (2 slices, 2 oz)	205
chicken	
breast (½, no skin, 4 oz)	140-160
drumstick (1, no skin, 3 oz)	75-80
thigh (1, no skin, 3 oz)	105-115
wing (1, with skin)	80-100
McDonald's McNuggets (6 pieces)	314
Kentucky Fried Chicken (2 pieces)	661
frankfurter (2 oz)	
with roll	170
lamb (3 oz)	
chop	160-305
leg	160-235
pork	
bacon (2 slices)	60-85
chop (3 oz)	230-335
ham (3 oz)	160-245
roast (3 oz)	215-310
salami (uncooked, ⅔ oz, 2 slices)	85
turkey (3 oz, no skin)	
light meat	135-150
dark meat	160-175

Pasta and Grain (¾ cup)	**Calories**
macaroni (cooked)	
plain	115-145
with cheese	175-325
noodles	150
pancake (1, 4" diameter, plain)	60
rice (cooked)	135-175
rice cake (one)	35

spaghetti (cooked)	
plain	115-145
in tomato sauce, with cheese	140-195
with meat balls	195-250
waffle (1, 7″ diameter)	245

Popcorn (1 cup, popped)	**Calories**
air popped	30-50
popped in oil	55-75
sugar-syrup coated	135
popcorn ball	150-200

Seafood	**Calories**
bluefish (baked, 3 oz)	135
crabmeat (3 oz, ½ cup)	80
mackerel (broiled with fat, 3 oz)	200
oysters (raw, ½ cup)	80
salmon (broiled or baked, 3 oz)	155
salmon (canned, pink, 3 oz)	150
sardines (canned in oil, drained, 3 oz)	170
shrimp (3 oz)	100
tuna (canned in oil, drained, 3 oz)	165
tuna (canned in water, drained 3 oz)	100-110
McDonald's Filet-O-Fish	432
Burger King Whaler	540
Wendy's Fish Filet	365

Soups (one cup)	**Calories**
bean with bacon	175
beef noodle	70-85
bouillon	15
chicken gumbo	55
chicken noodle	62-75
chicken with rice	50-60
clam chowder (Manhattan)	80
cream of mushroom (made with water)	135

cream of mushroom (made with milk)	215
minestrone	85-105
pea (made with water)	130
pea (made with milk)	213
tomato (made with water)	85
tomato (made with milk)	160-175

Vegetables	**Calories**
asparagus (cooked, 1 cup)	36
broccoli (cooked, 1 cup)	40-50
brussels sprouts (cooked, 1 cup)	50-55
cabbage (½ cup)	10
carrot (1 medium, ½ cup)	25-30
cauliflower (1 cup)	30
celery (three 5″ stalks)	10
corn, sweet (1 cup, kernels)	135
corn, sweet (1 ear)	85-122
cucumber (6 center slices, ⅛″ thick)	5
eggplant (1 cup)	25-40
green beans (1 cup)	30-35
lettuce (wedge, 1/6 head)	10
lettuce (½ cup, shredded or chopped)	5
lima beans (½ cup)	95
mushrooms (1 cup)	20-25
okra (cooked, 1 cup)	45
onion (1 cup)	40-60
peas (½ cup)	65
pepper, green (1 medium)	15
potato	
baked with skin (8 oz.)	170
boiled without skin (8 oz)	150
french fried (10 pieces)	110-215
spinach (cooked, ½ cup)	25
spinach (raw, 2 cups)	28
squash (summer, ½ cup)	15
squash (winter, ½ cup)	45-65
sweet potato (1, baked with skin, peeled, 6-7 oz)	115
tomato (2½″ diameter)	20

Miscellaneous Foods	Calories
Butter Buds (1 tbsp)	6
catsup (1 tbsp)	15
corn chips (1 cup)	230
crackers, graham (1)	30
crackers, saltine (4)	50
doughnut	120-150
egg (hard-boiled, large)	80
egg (fried in fat)	100
Egg Beaters (¼ cup = 1 egg)	30
margarine (1 pat: 1 x 1/3")	35
margarine (1 tbsp)	100
mayonnaise, regular (1 tbsp)	100
mayonnaise, diet (1 tbsp)	40
peanut butter (1 tbsp)	95
pie (1 slice, 1/6 pie)	
apple	405
cherry	410
pecan	575
pumpkin	320
pizza (plain, ⅛ of 14" diameter)	150-250
potato chips (10 pieces)	115
pretzel, Dutch (1)	60
pretzel sticks (5 regular)	10
taco (1)	160-195
tofu (3½ oz)	70

Adams, C.F. *Nutritive Value of American Foods in Common Units.* Agricultural Handbook No. 456, Agricultural Research Service, U.S. Department of Agriculture, U.S. Government Printing Office: Washington, D.C. 1975.

Calories and Weight: The USDA Pocket Guide. Agriculture Information Bulletin No. 364, U.S. Government Printing Office: Washington, D.C., 1981.

Nutritive Value of Foods. Home and Garden Bulletin No. 72, U.S. Government Printing Office, Washington, D.C., 1981.

McDonald's Corp., Burger King Corp., Wendy's International.

G/MAKING A WATER WHEEL*

To help you remember to drink at least six glasses of water per day and keep track of what you've had, here's how to make a "water wheel."

1. Cut out the square and circle. Paste on thin cardboard.
2. Cut the shapes out again. (Optional: Stick on transparent plastic to make the wheel more durable.)
3. Make a hole through the center of each. Fasten the circle to the square at their centers with a round-headed clip.
4. Tape the two metal legs of the clip against the back of the square. This will keep them from slipping when the wheel is turned to line up the arrow with the desired number.

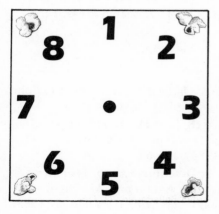

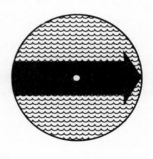

*Suggested and developed by Dr. Ira Herskowitz

H/BIBLIOGRAPHY

1 HOW I GOT FAT AND WHAT I LEARNED FROM IT

Elting, L.M. and Isenberg, S. *You Can Be Fat-Free Forever.* New York: Penguin Books, 1974.

Jordan, H.A., Levitz, L.S. and Kimbrell, G.M. *Eating Is Okay!* New York: Signet, 1976.

Stuart, R.B. and Davis, B. *Slim Chance in a Fat World: Behavioral Control Of Obesity.* Champaign, Illinois: Research Press, 1972.

2 WHY LOSE WEIGHT?

Aronson, V. *A Practical Guide to Optimal Nutrition.* Boston: John Wright/PSG Inc. 1983, p. 58.

Burton, B.T., Foster, W.R., Hirsch, J., et al. "Health Implications of Obesity: An NIH Consensus Development Conference." *International Journal of Obesity* 9 (1985): 155-69.

Colvin, R.H. and Olson, S.B. "A Descriptive Analysis of Men and Women Who Have Lost Significant Weight and Are Highly Successful at Maintaining the Loss." *Addictive Behaviors* 8 (1983): 287-95.

Harrison, G.G. "Height-Weight Tables." *Annals of Internal Medicine* 103 (1985): 989-94.

Hirsch, J., Bell, C.H., Dwyer, J.T., et al. "Health Implications of Obesity. National Institutes of Health Consensus Development Conference Statement. *Annals of Internal Medicine* 103 (1985): 1073-77.

Kolata, G. "Obesity Declared a Disease." *Science* 227 (1985): 1019-20.

Metropolitan Life Foundation. 1983 Metropolitan Height and Weight Tables. Statistical Bulletin 64 (1983): 2-9.

Stunkard, A.J., Sorensen, T.I.A., Hanis, C., et al. "An Adoption Study of Human Obesity." *New England Journal of Medicine* 314 (1986): 193-98.

Van Itallie, T.B. "Health Implications of Overweight and Obesity in the United States." *Annals of Internal Medicine* 103 (1975): 983-88.

——— "Bad News and Good News about Obesity." *New England Journal of Medicine* 314 (1986): 239-40.

Wadden, T.A., Stunkard, A.J. "Social and Psychological Consequences of Obesity." *Annals of Internal Medicine* 103 (1985): 1062-67.

3 THE MOUNT EVEREST APPROACH AND OTHER PATTERNS OF OVEREATING

Bruch, H. "Conceptual Confusion in Eating Disorders." *Journal of Nervous and Mental Disease* 133 (1961): 46-54.

Lowe, M.G. "The Role of Anticipated Deprivation in Overeating." *Addictive Behaviors* 7 (1982): 103-12.

4 THE POPCORN-PLUS DIET: HOW IT WORKS

Wurtman J.J. and Wurtman, R.J. "D-fenfluramine Selectively Decreases Carbohydrate but Not Protein Intake in Obese Subjects." *International Journal of Obesity* 8 (suppl. 1) (1984): 79-84.

5 MEET POPCORN!

Carper, J. and Krause, P.A. *The All-in-One Calorie Counter.* New York: Bantam, 1974.

Hoseney, R.C., Zeleznak, K. and Abdelrahman, A. "Mechanism of Popcorn Popping." *Journal of Cereal Science* 1 (1983): 43-52.

Kusche, L. *Popcorn.* Tucson, Arizona: HPBooks, 1977.

Lafavore, M. "Garden Gourmet Popcorn." *Organic Gardening,* October 1983, p. 28.

Pennington, J.A.T. and Church, H.N. *Bowes and Church's Food Values of Portions Commonly Used.* Philadelphia: J.B. Lippincott Company, 1980, p. 71.

Selsam, M.E. *Popcorn.* New York: William Morrow and Company, 1976.

United States Department of Agriculture: *Nutritive Value of Foods.* Home and Garden Bulletin No. 72. Washington, D.C., 1981.

Van Itallie, T.B. "Dietary Approaches to the Treatment of Obesity." In *Obesity,* edited by A.J. Stunkard. Philadelphia: W.B. Saunders, 1980, p. 253.

Woodside, D. *What Makes Popcorn Pop?* New York: Atheneum, 1980.

Wurtman, J.J. *The Carbohydrate Craver's Diet.* New York: Ballantine Books, 1983, p. 38.

6 GOAL SETTING: THE FRAMEWORK

Bandura, A. "Self-Efficacy: Toward a Unifying Theory of Behavioral Change. *Psychological Review* 84 (1977): 191-215.

Bandura, A. and Schunk, D.H. "Cultivating Competence, Self-Efficacy, and Intrinsic Interest Through Proximal Self-Motivation." *Journal of Personality and Social Psychology* 41 (1981): 586-98.

Barnett, M.L. and Stanicek, J.A. "Effects of Goal Setting on Achievement in Archery." *Research Quarterly* 50 (1979): 328-332.

Hill, N. *Think and Grow Rich.* New York: Fawcett Crest, 1960.

Lakein, A. *How to Get Control of Your Time and Your Life.* New York: Signet, 1973.

Meyer, P.J. *Power of Goal Setting* (cassette). SMC: Waco, Texas.

7 LOSING WEIGHT THE POPCORN-PLUS DIET WAY

Consumer Reports "Corn Poppers" November, 1979, pp.628-31.

8 KEEPING IT OFF: YOUR NEW GOAL

Colvin, R.H. and Olson, S.B. "A Descriptive Analysis of Men and Women Who Have Lost Significant Weight and Are Highly Successful at Maintaining the Loss." *Addictive Behaviors* 8 (1983): 287-95.

Cooper, K.H. "The Fitness Factor in Total Well-Being." In *The Aerobics Program for Total Well-Being.* Toronto: Bantam Books, 1982, pp. 105-36.

Henderson, J. *The Long Run Solution.* Mountain View, California: World Publications, 1976.

Marston, A.R. and Criss, J. "Maintenance of Successful Weight Loss: Incidence and Prediction." *International Journal of Obesity* 8 (1984): 435-39.

Paffenbarger, R.S. Jr., et al. "Physical Activity, All-Cause Mortality, and Longevity of College Alumni. *New England Journal of Medicine* 314 (1986): 605-13.

9 BEHAVIORAL TOOLS FOR MAINTENANCE

Jordan, H.A., Levitz, L.S. and Kimbrell, G.M. *Eating Is Okay!* New York: New American Library, 1976.

Kromhout, D., Bosschieter, E.B., et al. "The Inverse Relation Between Fish Consumption and 20-Year Mortality from Coronary Heart Disease." *New England Journal of Medicine* 312 (1985): 1205-09.

Phillipson, B.E., Rothrock, D.W., et al. "Reduction of Plasma Lipids, Lipoproteins, and Apoproteins by Dietary Fish Oils in Patients with Hypertriglyceridemia." *New England Journal of Medicine* 312 (1985): 1210-16.

Stuart, R.B. "Behavioral Control of Overeating." *Behavior Research and Therapy* 5 (1967): 357-365.

10 THE POPCORN-PLUS DIET AND YOUR CHILDREN

Brody, J. *Jane Brody's Nutrition Book.* New York: Bantam Books, 1981.

Bruch, H. "Conceptual Confusion in Eating Disorders." *Journal of Nervous and Mental Disease* 133 (1961): 46-54.

DeClements, B. *Nothing's Fair in Fifth Grade.* New York: Scholastic Inc, 1981.

Dietz, W.H., Jr. "Childhood Obesity: Susceptibility, Cause, and Management." *Journal of Pediatrics* 103 (1983): 676-86.

Epstein, L.H., Wing, R.R., et al. "Effect of Diet and Controlled Exercise on Weight Loss in Obese Children." *Journal of Pediatrics* 107 (1985): 358-61.

——— "Childhood Obesity." *Pediatric Clinics of North America* 32 (1985):363-79.

Garn, S.M. "Continuities and Changes in Fatness from Infancy Through Adulthood." *Current Problems in Pediatrics* 15 (1985):6-47.

Glueck, C.J. "Pediatric Primary Prevention of Atherosclerosis." *New England Journal of Medicine* 314 (1986):175-77.

Harris, C.S., Baker, S.P., et al. "Childhood Asphyxiation by Food: A National Analysis and Overview." *Journal of the American Medical Association* 251 (1984): 2231-2235.

Herskowitz, J. and Rosman, N.P. "Disorders of Eating and Elimination." In *Pediatrics, Neurology, and Psychiatry—Common Ground.* New York: Macmillan, 1982, pp. 227-77.

Jacobson, Mary "The Complete Eater's Digest and Nutrition Scoreboard." New York. Anchor Press, (1985).

Johnston, F.E. "Health Implications of Childhood Obesity." *Annals of Internal Medicine* 103 (1985): 1068-72.

Kolata, G. "Obese Children: A Growing Problem." *Science* 232 (1986): 20-21.

Minderaa, R.B. and Wit, J.M. "Behaviour Therapy of Obese Children and Results 21 Months After Treatment." *International Journal of Obesity* 7 (1983): 143-52.

Mofenson, H.C. and Greensher, J. "Management of the Choking Child." *Pediatric Clinics of North America* 32 (1985): 183-92.

Stunkard, A.J., Sorensen, T.I.A., et al. "An Adoption Study of Human Obesity." *New England Journal of Medicine* 314 (1986): 193-198.

U.S. Department of Agriculture: *Ideas for Better Eating.* Science and Education Administration/Human Nutrition, U.S. Government Printing Office, Superintendent of Documents: Washington, DC, 1981.

U.S. Department of Agriculture: *Eating for Better Health.* Food and Nutrition Service, Program Aid No. 1290. U.S. Government Printing Office, Superintendent of Documents: Washington, DC, 1981.

Waxman, M. and Stunkard, A.J. "Caloric Intake and Expenditure of Obese Boys." *Journal of Pediatrics* 96 (1980): 187-193.

11 ANSWERS TO DIETERS' QUESTIONS

Bick, P.A. "Seasonal Major Affective Disorder." *American Journal of Psychiatry* 143 (1986): 90-91.

Bray, G.A. "Drugs in the Treatment of Obesity." In *Nutritional Support of Medical Practice,* 2nd edition, edited by H.A. Schneider, C.E. Anderson, D.B. Cousin. Philadelphia: Harper and Row, 1983, pp 482-85.

Bruch, H. *The Golden Cage: The Enigma of Anorexia Nervosa.* Cambridge: Harvard University Press, 1978.

Herzog, D.B. and Copeland, P.M. "Eating Disorders." *New England Journal of Medicine* 313 (1985): 295-301.

Rosenthal, N.E., Sack, D.A., Carpenter, C.J., et al. "Antidepressant Effects of Light in Seasonal Affective Disorder." *American Journal of Psychiatry* 142 (1985):163-70.

Stunkard, A.J., and Stellar, E. (Eds.) *Eating and Its Disorders.* New York: Raven Press, 1984.

APPENDIX B: 21 DAYS OF MEALS FOR WEIGHT LOSS

Gilliard, J. and Kirkpatrick, J. *The Guiltless Gourmet.* Nutrition Wise: Box 499, Rancho Mirage, California 92270, 1983.

United States Department of Agriculture: *Eating for Better Health.* Food and Nutrition Service, Program Aid No. 1290, U.S. Government Printing Office: Washington, DC, 1981.
United States Department of Agriculture: *Ideas for Better Eating.* Science and Education Administration/Human Nutrition. U.S. Government Printing Office: Washington, DC 1981.

APPENDIX C: SCHOOL LUNCHES AND SNACKS

Kusche, L. *Popcorn.* Tucson, Arizona: HPBooks Inc., 1977.
United States Department of Agriculture: *Eating for Better Health.* Food and Nutrition Service, Program Aid No. 1290, U.S. Government Printing Office: Washington, DC, 1981.
United States Department of Agriculture: *Ideas for Better Eating.* Science and Education Administration/Human Nutrition. U.S. Government Printing Office: Washington, DC 1981.

APPENDIX D: POPCORN RECIPES

Kusche, L. *Popcorn.* Tucson, Arizona: HPBooks Inc., 1977.

APPENDIX F: CALORIC CONTENT OF EVERYDAY FOODS

Adams, C.F.: *Nutritive Value of American Foods in Common Units.* Agriculural Research Service, U.S. Department of Agriculture, Agriculture Handbook No. 456. U.S. Government Printing Office: Washington, DC 1975.
Gebhardt, S.E. and Matthews, R.H. *Nutritive Value of Foods.* U.S. Department of Agriculture, Human Nutrition Information Service, Home and Garden Bulletin No. 72. U.S. Government Printing Office: Washington, DC 1981.
United States Department of Agriculture: *Calories & Weight.* Science and Education Administratin, Agriculture Information Bulletin No. 364. U.S. Government Printing Office: Washington, DC 1981.

INDEX